She Writes

Visions and Voices of Seaside Scribes

Kathleen L. Martens
Literary Arts Curator and Editor

Salt Water
MEDIA

29 Broad Street, Suite 104
Berlin, MD 21811
www.saltwatermedia.com

Copyright © 2018 Kathleen Langmaack Martens

Published by
Saltwater Media, Inc.
29 Broad Street, Suite 104
Berlin, MD 21811
www.saltwatermedia.com

All rights reserved. This book or any portion thereof may not be reproduced or used in any manner whatsoever without the express written permission of the publisher except for the use of brief quotations in a book review.

Printed in the United States of America
Library of Congress Number: 2018949838
ISBN: 978-1-62806-180-2

PERMISSIONS AND COPYRIGHTS
Cover Design: by Crystal Heidel. © 2018 by Crystal Heidel
Book Design: by Diane Buric. © 2018 by Diane Buric

CONTENT COPYRIGHTS
"Authenticity," Ruth Wanberg-Alcorn. © 2018 by Ruth M. Alcorn.
    Reprinted with permission.
"Freedom Yearning," Ruth Wanberg-Alcorn. © 2018 by Ruth M. Alcorn.
    Reprinted with permission.
"She's Come Undone," Ash'iz "Tha Rebirth." © 2018 by Ashley Cuffee.
    Reprinted with permission.
"Columbus Day," Sarah Barnett. © 2012 by Sarah Barnett.
    Reprinted with permission.
"Sadie's Legacy," Sarah Barnett. © 2013 by Sarah Barnett.
    Reprinted with permission.
"Talking with My Mother," Sarah Barnett. © 2017 by Sarah Barnett.
    Reprinted with permission.
"What We Steal," Sarah Barnett. © 2012 by Sarah Barnett.
    Reprinted with permission.
"Supper," Jane O'Rourke Bender. © 2016 by Jane O'Rourke Bender.
    Reprinted with permission.

"Letter to the Deities," Jane O'Rourke Bender. © 2016
by Jane O'Rourke Bender. Reprinted with permission.

"Poem for Henry," Jane O'Rourke Bender. © 2016
by Jane O'Rourke Bender. Reprinted with permission.

"Dancing in the Venetian Rain," Kimberly Blanch. © 2018
by Kimberly Marie Blanch. Reprinted with permission.

"Return Ticket," Christy Walker Briedis. © 2018 by Helen Christine
Walker Briedis. Reprinted with permission.

"Autism Abridged," Cynthia Gratz Campbell. © 2018 by Cynthia Gratz
Campbell. Reprinted with permission.

"The Snow Party," Judy Catterton. © 2018 by Judy Catterton.
Reprinted with permission.

"The Runaway," Judy Catterton. © 2018 by Judy Catterton.
Reprinted with permission.

"We Women of a Certain Age," Judy Catterton. © 2016
by Judy Catterton. Reprinted with permission.

"Marina's Wish," Terri Clifton. © 2018 by Terri Clifton.
Reprinted with permission.

"Tadasana—Mountain Pose," Ellen Collins. © 2017 by Ellen Collins.
Reprinted with permission.

"Parkland in February," Ellen Collins. © 2018 by Ellen Collins.
Reprinted with permission.

"When the Universe Opens," Ellen Collins. © 2015 by Ellen Collins.
Reprinted with permission.

"Vrksasana—Tree Pose," Ellen Collins. © 2017 by Ellen Collins.
Reprinted with permission.

"Advice from a Hummingbird," Gail Braune Comorat. © 2018
by Gail Braune Comorat. Reprinted with permission.

"She Writes," Gail Braune Comorat. © 2018 by Gail Braune Comorat.
Reprinted with permission.

"What Happens at Sephora," Gail Braune Comorat. © 2015
by Gail Braune Comorat. Reprinted with permission.

"Hard-Earned Wisdoms," Ginny Daly. © 2018 by Ginny Daly.
Reprinted with permission.

"The Long Goodbye," Ginny Daly. © 2004 by Ginny Daly.
Reprinted with permission.

"Specimen A," Kelsey Dugan. © 2018 by Kelsey Dugan.
Reprinted with permission.

"Death," Mimi S Dupont. © 2018 by Mary S Dupont.
Reprinted with permission.

"Enfolded," Mimi S Dupont. © 2018 by Mary S Dupont.
   Reprinted with permission.
"Logjam," Mimi S Dupont. © 2018 by Mary S Dupont.
   Reprinted with permission.
"Risk," Mimi S Dupont. © 2018 by Mary S Dupont.
   Reprinted with permission.
"Writing About Our Darkness," Mimi S Dupont. © 2018
   by Mary S Dupont. Reprinted with permission.
"The Gift of Hope," Beth Ewell. © 2018 by Beth Ewell.
   Reprinted with permission.
"Angels in the Sand," Linda Federman. © 2018 by Linda Federman.
   Reprinted with permission.
"Another Mother," Irene Fick. © 2018 by Irene Terese Fick.
   Reprinted with permission.
"Dancing Queen," Irene Fick. © 2018 by Irene Terese Fick.
   Reprinted with permission.
"Old Woman Sleeps," Irene Fick. © 2018 by Irene Terese Fick.
   Reprinted with permission.
"Spinning at the Midway Gym," Irene Fick. © 2018 by Irene Terese Fick.
   Reprinted with permission.
"Lost and Found Again," Stephanie Fowler. © 2018 by Stephanie Fowler.
   Reprinted with permission.
"Beluga Pangaea," Katherine Gekker. © 2018 by Katherine Gekker.
   Reprinted with permission.
"Lessons Learned: Taking Care of Myself," Lisa Graff. © 2018
   by Lisa Graff. Reprinted with permission.
"Fall in Love with a Woman Who Writes," Crystal Heidel. © 2016
   by Crystal Sue Heidel. Reprinted with permission.
"fog," jahill. © 2018 by Jane A. Hill. Reprinted with permission.
"dance, jahill. © 2018 by Jane A. Hill. Reprinted with permission.
"storm," jahill. © 2018 by Jane A. Hill. Reprinted with permission.
"The Photograph on the Wall," Margaret Farrell Kirby. © 2018 by
   Margaret Farrell Kirby. Reprinted with permission.
"How to Fall in Love with a Woman," Jane Klein. © 2018
   by D. Jane Klein. Reprinted with permission.
"She and I," Jane Klein. © 2018 by D. Jane Klein.
   Reprinted with permission.

"Mary Woodwell Corbett Fowler," Mary Leach. © 2018 by Mary Leach. Reprinted with permission.

"Mother," Faith Lord. © 2018 by M. Faith Lord. Reprinted with permission.

"Grandma's Pork Dinner," Faith Lord. © 2018 by M. Faith Lord. Reprinted with permission.

"Point Pleasant," Faith Lord. © 2018 by M. Faith Lord. Reprinted with permission.

"Half of Two is My Only One," Kathleen L. Martens. © 2018 by Kathleen Langmaack Martens. Reprinted with permission.

"The Real Me," Kathleen L. Martens. © 2017 by Kathleen Langmaack Martens. Reprinted with permission.

"Funeral for a Pronoun," Rita B. Nelson. © 2018 by Rita B. Nelson. Reprinted with permission.

"hurting heart," Annie Plowman. © 2018 by Annie Plowman. Reprinted with permission.

"Outside the Lines," Annie Plowman. © 2018 by Annie Plowman. Reprinted with permission.

"THIS IS FOR US: international women's day," Annie Plowman. © 2018 by Annie Plowman. Reprinted with permission.

"Call Back," Carole Schauer. © 2018 by Carole Schauer. Reprinted with permission.

"Side by Side," Carole Schauer. © 2018 by Carole Schauer. Reprinted with permission.

"A Cougar at the Starboard, Dewey Beach," Nancy Powichroski Sherman. © 2014 by Nancy Powichroski Sherman. Reprinted with permission.

"A Beautiful Nothing," Irene Wanberg. © 2018 by Irene Emily Wanberg. Reprinted with permission.

"Dancing with Strangers," Marjorie F. Weber. © 2018 by Marjorie F. Weber. Reprinted with permission.

"Office Politics," Marjorie F. Weber. © 2018 by Marjorie F. Weber. Reprinted with permission.

"The Water's Edge," Katherine Winfield. © 2018 by Katherine Winfield. Reprinted with permission.

"Another History of Childhood," Judy Wood. © 2018 by Judy Wood. Reprinted with permission.

"Doors," Judy Wood. © 2018 by Judy Wood. Reprinted with permission.

"Daughter," Sherri Wright. © 2018 by Sharon KB Wright. Reprinted with permission.
"Girls on the Street," Sherri Wright © 2018 by Sharon KB Wright. Reprinted with permission.
"Waiting for Sunrise," Sherri Wright © 2013 by Sharon KB Wright. Reprinted with permission.
"Why She Never Asked Why," Sherri Wright © 2018 by Sharon KB Wright. Reprinted with permission.

Contents

Acknowledgements..................................11
Preface, Kathleen L. Martens, Curator and Editor.............. 13

She writes because it is her addiction
because all her life   she has hoarded words
    and now they are spilling out

She Writes, *Gail Braune Comorat*......................17
Fall in Love with a Woman Who Writes, *Crystal Heidel*.......... 19
The Runaway, *Judy Catterton*......................... 23
The Real Me, *Kathleen L. Martens*...................... 25
Why She Never Asked Why, *Sherri Wright*...................37
Lost and Found Again, *Stephanie Fowler* 39
Tadasana—Mountain Pose, *Ellen Collins*....................45
Vrksasana—Tree Pose, *Ellen Collins* 47
Logjam, *Mimi S Dupont*............................ 49
Poem for Henry, *Jane O'Rourke Bender*......................51

She writes because
    her sisters are hurting
because she has no other way
    to comfort them
        but with her words

Columbus Day, *Sarah Barnett* 55
Girls on the Street, *Sherri Wright*.......................61
Dancing with Strangers, *Marjorie F. Weber* 63
Call Back, *Carole Schauer*............................67
Risk, *Mimi S Dupont*.............................. 69
Spinning at the Midway Gym, *Irene Fick*.....................71
Side by Side, *Carole Schauer*.......................... 73
Advice from a Hummingbird, *Gail Braune Comorat* 75

She writes
because her mother is gone
  and their conversation still goes on

The Photograph on the Wall, *Margaret Farrell Kirby* 79
Another Mother, *Irene Fick*. 85
Mother, *Faith Lord*. 87
Daughter, *Sherri Wright* 93
Beluga Pangaea, *Katherine Gekker* 95
The Gift of Hope, *Beth Ewell*. 97
Old Woman Sleeps, *Irene Fick* 101
Grandma's Pork Dinner, *Faith Lord* 103

She writes to make sense of the world
because some days
  she is in a dark place
  and words are the only way out

Writing About our Darkness, *Mimi S Dupont* 107
Angels in the Sand, *Linda Federman*. 109
hurting heart, *Annie Plowman* 115
The Pond, *Rosa M. Fernández* 117
fog, *jahill* 121
Authenticity, *Ruth Wanberg-Alcorn*. 123
A Beautiful Nothing, *Irene Emily Wanberg*. 125

She writes to keep her brother alive
She writes because when she feels alone
  writing consoles her

Doors, *Judy Wood*. 129
Talking with My Mother, *Sarah Barnett*. 133
The Long Goodbye, *Ginny Daly*. 135
Point Pleasant, *Faith Lord*. 137
dance, *jahill*. 141
Letter to the Deities, *Jane O'Rourke Bender* 143
The Water's Edge, *Katherine Winfield*. 145

She writes to give shape to things
she will never understand

Autism Abridged, *Cynthia Gratz Campbell*.....................151
Outside the Lines, *Annie Plowman*..........................157
Sadie's Legacy, *Sarah Barnett*..............................159
Specimen A, *Kelsey Dugan*..................................163
Funeral for a Pronoun, *Rita B. Nelson*.......................165
storm, *jahill*..169
What Happens at Sephora, *Gail Braune Comorat*...............173
Half of Two Is My Only One, *Kathleen L. Martens*.............175

She writes with renewed faith
because she wants to remember
to honor
because she is a witness

Return Ticket, *Christy Walker Briedis*........................181
Hard-Earned Wisdoms, *Ginny Daly*..........................191
What We Steal, *Sarah Barnett*..............................193
Parkland in February, *Ellen Collins*..........................195
Another History of Childbirth, *Judy Wood*...................197
Supper, *Jane O'Rourke Bender*..............................201
Mary Woodwell Corbett Fowler, *Mary Leach*..................203
When the Universe Opens, *Ellen Collins*......................209

She writes and writes
because the stories won't stop
because writing is her way of dancing
it is how she keeps breathing

The Snow Party, *Judy Catterton*.............................213
Marina's Wish, *Terri Clifton*................................215
Dancing Queen, *Irene Fick*..................................221
Dancing in the Venetian Rain, *Kimberly Blanch*...............223
Lessons Learned: Taking Care of Myself, *Lisa Graff*............225
A Cougar at the Starboard, Dewey Beach, Delaware,
   Nancy Powichroski Sherman..............................229

She writes to celebrate
     and to mourn
She will not be silenced

Waiting for Sunrise, *Sherri Wright* 239
How to Fall in Love with a Woman, *Jane Klein* 241
She and I, *Jane Klein* 243
She's Come Undone, *Ash'iz "Tha Rebirth"* .247
Death, *Mimi S Dupont* 251
Freedom Yearning, *Ruth Wanberg-Alcorn* 253
We Women of a Certain Age, *Judy Catterton* 257
Office Politics, *Marjorie F. Weber* 259
THIS IS FOR US: international women's day, *Annie Plowman* 261
Enfolded, *Mimi S Dupont* 263

Author Biographies 265

Acknowledgments

A resounding *thank you* to Deborah Rolig, visionary and tireless supporter of women in the arts for her unique idea to include a book as the literary arts component of the *SHE* arts exhibition, held September 2018 at the Ocean City Center for the Arts. The authors and readers of *She Writes: Visions and Voices of Seaside Scribes* are grateful for her progressive thinking and creativity. And because of Deb, last year's award-winning book, *The Divine Feminine: An Anthology of Seaside Scribes*, now has a sequel to allow our collective vision to live on. Our deepest gratitude to artist Diane Gray for her behind-the-scenes support.

A heartfelt thanks to all of the Seaside Scribes, authors of *She Writes*, who entrusted their works to this endeavor to reach readers and raise funds for scholarships for writing at the Rehoboth Beach Writers Guild and programs at the Ocean City Center for the Arts to empower women through the healing aspects of artistic self-expression and creativity.

Cheers and gratitude for the *She Writes* Editorial Team. The unsung heroes in a book's life are those people who have the talent and eyes to bring each piece to the page in its best light. Thank you all for making this book possible. Poets—Gail Braune Comorat and Ellen Collins. Essay and short story reviewers—Sarah Barnett and Judy Catterton. Final manuscript reviewer—Mimi Dupont; and Christy Briedis for her support in structuring and sequencing *She Writes*.

Applause, applause for Rina Thaler, Executive Director of The Art League of Ocean City Center for the Arts, for providing the encouragement and magnificent water-side venue for the month-long women's arts exhibition, *SHE*. Her spirit is a force for the entire community.

For her patience and talent in designing the pages and bringing together the book, the *She Writes* authors thank Diane Buric, Diane Buric Design. www.DianeBuricDesign.com

Thank you to the multi-talented Crystal Heidel for our beautiful, impactful cover design. Writer, creator, designer, she is also an author in *She Writes*. crystalheidel.wordpress.com

Stephanie Fowler of Salt Water Media, Inc. Berlin, Maryland also wore two hats—Printer/Publisher extraordinaire and author of one of the works in *She Writes*. Thank you for being the ever-faithful, hand-holding guide for authors—emerging and seasoned—to release their works to the world. www.saltwatermedia.com

Maribeth Fischer, Executive Director of the Rehoboth Beach Writers' Guild is the backbone of the writing community in Southern Coastal

Delaware. Any writer who has been mentored, taught, or has basked in the light of this extraordinary woman is inspired and transformed. www.rehobothbeachwritersguild.com

Thank you, Ruth Wanberg-Alcorn, founder of the Ocean City Library Writers Group, for connecting the editor of *She Writes* with the authors from the Maryland shore and for contributing her words to this endeavor.

Deep gratitude to my husband, Steuart, for his unending support for everything I choose to do.

Preface

"There is no greater agony than bearing an untold story inside you."
—Maya Angelou

Why do you hold this book in your hands right now? Because *She Writes*. She who pushes aside all else to compose, scratch-out, highlight, delete and re-write late into the night or until the glow of the morning insists its way around her bedroom shades—she writes for you.

Writing can be a lonely art form. If she's fortunate, when a writer gives voice to her experiences, dreams, pains and thoughts, they will travel in print to the eyes and minds of a stranger—a man in Manhattan who wants to understand his lover; a woman alone in Wyoming; a graduate student seeking answers for her life; a beleaguered soul on a bus to Boston needing a jump-start to the day; or a voracious reader on a beach in Hawaii devouring everything in sight.

Writers rarely get to see or hear the reader's reaction. Yet, still, they write in hopes their words will touch someone, teach someone, make someone laugh, cry, relate, change their mind, or simply de-stress.

I've witnessed the poignant and sometimes life-changing influence of the writer-reader experience—a kind of alchemy that can transform a reader with the right words at the right time. I don't underestimate what this anthology might do for you. As a reader you might grow, catch insights, empathize and internalize the lessons in the stories for your own life.

This is the intimate gift from the unseen writer to the unknown reader.

She Writes: Visions and Voices of Seaside Scribes is structured using the stanzas of the opening poem, "She Writes." Each section serves up a variety of insightful essays, engaging short stories, and evocative poems from the pens of the Seaside Scribes—women writers from the Delaware and Maryland coasts.

The magic of an anthology means there's a broad spectrum of lived experiences, styles, and perspectives, and no shortage of ways to connect with dozens of writers' words. A book to keep on your nightstand that might just light up your day or put you to sleep—well, in a good way—to become the stuff of your dreams.

This is why *She Writes*.

Good Reading,

Kathleen L. Martens
Literary Arts Curator and Editor

A sequel to *The Divine Feminine: An Anthology of Seaside Scribes*—*She Writes: Visions and Voices of Seaside Scribes* served as the literary arts component for a month-long women's arts exhibition in September 2018, titled, *SHE,* at the Art League of Ocean City, Center for the Arts, curated by Deborah Rolig. 100% of the profits from book sales will go to charities empowering women through the arts.

She writes because it is her addiction
because all her life   she has hoarded words
and now they are spilling out

She Writes

She writes because it is her addiction
because all her life   she has hoarded words
      and now they are spilling out

She writes because
      her sisters are hurting
because she has no other way
      to comfort them
           but with her words

She writes
because her mother is gone
      and their conversation still goes on

She writes to make sense of the world
because some days
      she is in a dark place
      and words are the only way out

She writes to keep her brother alive
She writes because when she feels alone
      writing consoles her

She writes to give shape to things
      she will never understand

She writes with renewed faith
      because she wants to remember
           to honor
because she is a witness

She writes and writes
because the stories won't stop
        because writing is her way of dancing
        it is how she keeps breathing

She writes to celebrate
        and to mourn
She will not be silenced

Gail Braune Comorat

Fall in Love with a Woman Who Writes

Crystal Heidel

Fall in love with a woman who understands the power of the written word, how they can twist and tempt, for she will tell you exactly how she feels, especially when she's alone with you. She may whisper it to you in the middle of the night when the lights are out and she can only hear the sound of your breathing, even if you are sleeping. It may take her a little while to process her emotions, to think it all through, but she will tell you. And though it sounds like a contradiction, sometimes the words won't come easy for her and she'll say things she doesn't truly mean because she was fumbling through her thoughts, trying to piece together her emotions in the heat of the moment. It may take her days or weeks or months to figure something out, even if you've already forgotten all about it; because writers remember everything.

It's ingrained in them to remember. She'll pick out unique details and use them to set mood and emotion and setting. She'll use memories and moments from her life to write magically. She'll remember what you wore on your first date, the things you said, and the hints at the future. She'll remember how you may or may not have kissed her goodnight or may or may not have asked her to stay the night.

She'll remember the whispers at the bar as you leaned closer, the warmth of your breath, the gentle tone of your voice when you say "sweetheart" or "babe" or "darling." She'll remember the tender gesture of touching the small of her back or the top of her knee as you excuse yourself from the bar. She'll remember the seductive, midnight talks and embraces and for-lovers-ears-only phrases. She'll remember the ways you caressed her skin, and the feel of your lips on the back of her neck, or the fact that you don't like her hair in your face as you sleep.

A writer will remember all the beautiful things you told her, but also the ones that cut deep. She'll write about them—about you—because it's important to her. Because you're important to her. And she'll learn from her mistakes. They will change her as much as they changed what you thought of her.

And because of that, she'll work hard. She doesn't give up easily. She knows that the first draft is shit. She knows that not every sentence, not every well-placed word will end up in the final draft. She'll make cuts.

She'll delete words, rewrite entire paragraphs, and scrap entire chapters if it doesn't help the novel. She's willing to work on it until it gets better. And she'll apply this same philosophy to your relationship. *If* you give her the chance.

She'll grow and change and become malleable, learning how to connect with you on a deeper level. She'll think about how to do this because she cares about you. And she wants to grow with you so that when you're old and grey and doubting her love, she can pull out her journal and show you that she cherished all those moments—every fight, every laugh, every kiss.

Writers think things through carefully, with caution. Sometimes she'll even over-think. This is not a flaw. She thinks deeply about life, about love, about how things could be better. She thinks about how she can change herself to make the world better, to make your relationship with her better. She sees your highest potential and thinks of ways to bring that out of you, to make each day count for you and for her.

She wears her heart on her sleeve because she is attuned to how fragile life is and how each moment must be captured so as not to be lost or squandered. She writes about this because she is exploring life's mysteries. She sees beauty in the mundane world around her because she is, at heart, a romantic. Don't ever tell her she shouldn't be.

She will be vulnerable but that means she does not fear her emotions. She will feel them. She will allow them to pass through her and then she'll write about them. And some of them may even be about you, and they may or may not be nice or kind, but it is how she processes things. Don't think that just because you are in one of her written pieces that shows a different side of you, that her feelings for you have changed. She knows that you cannot fully love someone until you've seen their darkness. And if she still wants to be with you after she's seen it, don't let her go. That's rare today.

And though it seems it, she is not crazy. She may be eccentric. She may infuriate you on occasion, but her soul is filled with magic and adventure and beauty and a touch of madness. However, life with her will never be dull. She loves to learn and will always be willing to try something new. Because of this, she will always read. And the more she devours books the more she realizes she doesn't know everything and that just makes her insanely curious, craving knowledge. She cannot stop wanting to learn. So teach her something new. Talk about something she knows nothing about. Challenge her intelligence. This will make her love you more.

And yes, she will eventually choose writing over you. Be okay with that. Be okay when she's awake at 2 a.m. on a Tuesday morning, writing in her notebook with the lamp on in the living room, glasses she hardly wears perched on her nose, a blanket tucked close around her, so she doesn't disturb you. Chances are high that you were her inspiration. So let her write. She'll come back to bed, refreshed, clear-headed, happy, and ready to spend the rest of the night burrowed in your warmth. Because writing, like breathing, is the only way she can survive, which means she can be easily distressed, a little depressed or equally elated. So give her space, be supportive, but don't make accusations, because as gorgeous as her magical soul is, she can be dangerous.

Words are her weapon.

The Runaway

My son's first car was not his.
It was mine, a mustard-colored
Gremlin that disappeared
one night after an argument

when he ran away from home
to some mysterious place
where only teenagers go
a place of gnawing rage
and righteous rebellion
a place where hormonal
resentment bubbles up
with acid fury.

Does it matter what rule went too far;
what rein was held too tightly?
All I knew then was I had lost
my little boy: the boy who cried
when too few Valentine cards
filled the shoebox I covered
with scissored, pink paper hearts;
the boy Halloween found singing "Thriller"
and wearing one white sequined glove;
the boy whose face bled sunlight as
a soccer ball slammed home.

The night he drove away
I paced his room; stared
out his dormer window, willing
my Gremlin back to the driveway.
I lay in his bed of tangled sheets
and jumbled covers conjuring
the walls to whisper
his whereabouts.

He stayed away a week or so
and, though he never gave away his location,
he made certain his friend called
every night to tell me he was safe,
a sign I didn't realize then
was the promise of the
caring man he would one day become.

Judy Catterton

The Real Me

Kathleen L. Martens

Turning the photo toward the sunny window, I run my tremoring finger along its deckle edge. I recall the whiff of acrid aircraft fumes with a hint of my favorite fragrance whirling in the salty breeze around me. I hear the brass section playing that boogie-woogie beat, as the Back-up Babes and I jump in with our vocals just in time. We let out our wartime warbling with those tight harmonies and our boys in uniform spring to their feet. Those hundreds of sailor boys fling their white hats sky-high. I close my eyes and can see them—the unforgettable whirling Dixie Cups snowing down on us, sending chills down my arms. I feel my suspended wide smile at our encore and remember how it hurt my face.

"Eva Marie, oh my, we're stars." Janet, the alto in our trio, throws her head back and laughs. Half a century later the memory of her sounds of delight and the three of us jumping up and down hugging amidst the thunderous noise makes me beam. The stirring applause running down my spine—applause like the buzzing sound of incoming Douglas BTB Bombers performing perfect two-point-landings on our aircraft-carrier-stage.

I lower myself into the well-worn divot in the cobalt vinyl hospital chair with an audible puff and shuffle the stack of photos in my hands. It's good to be up and out of my hospital bed. The insulting scent of synthetic lemon hospital cleanser blended with the greasy inedible breakfast on my nearby tray accosts me. I want to forget where I am and be where I was.

That resounding applause from the sailors had roared past my days and faded in the distance like the thunder of the locomotive that used to rumble past my summer beach house and disappear into the horizon. Only the pitch of the nurses' voices rises now—no sailor hats, no ovation, no audience on their feet. The only stars I see now are the flickers of dust bouncing down the bands of sunlight through my venetian blinds. And who is that wizened widow in the dresser mirror who stares back at me? The less-than-full-step-down at my daughter's house had tripped me up. Weeks later here I sit, soft cast on my left leg; cast in a new role—invalid, aged, useless.

I want my life back. I'm not asking much—just walking daily on the beach, playing a sentimental tune on my piano to start my day, and my weak but weekly Bocce game at the club. Dear God, don't let me die in this place where I seem to fade away and disappear with each day.

The black and white photos in my hands don't begin to convey the palette of the person I was, or who I am. I'm from a long line of longevity, I want to argue; Great Grandmother Andrews pushed 104 in great health, sharp as a tack before her demise. But, sand is slipping through my hourglass, only a few specks of time left at the narrow neck of my remaining days, the doctors and nurses seem to think. I can't agree.

My daughter's strident voice floats outside my room. "Do you have to take that damned electronic device everywhere, Charlie? I thought you were coming to see your grandmother?"

"Mom, I *am* here to see Grandy."

"Well, I need to get to work. And she doesn't seem too chipper today, so don't upset her. She's not herself lately."

I see my grandson Charlie's nodding head through the rectangular wired-window in the oak door. I'm glad my daughter's off to work; she's loving but a bit bossy; I prefer the company of her son.

He cracks the door open. "Grandy. *Grandy?*"

Such a lovely moniker my grandson's chosen for me, "Grandy." I straighten the white waffle blanket across my lap. "Charlie, are you here for your daily story?" He's so sweet to listen. I'm such a bore with my relentless reminiscing, I think. I examine his Comic Con 2016 T-shirt and think of the hundreds of his favorite comics I've bought for him in past years—perfect, preserved in plastic, like new. Like I wish I were.

"Yeah, I want to know all your stories, Grandy." He props himself on the edge of the bed next to me, picks up the pile of photos from my nightstand and shuffles through them smiling. "These are so cool." Charlie looks over his shoulder at the nurses' station across the hall. "I don't get it."

"Get what?"

"Why they talk to you like that?"

"Like what?"

"You know, 'Oh, Mrs. Andrews have we had our pills today?' I hate that. What's with the *'we?'* I don't see *them* ever take any of those pills."

We laugh.

"It seems my aging causes vocal chords to tighten; makes people speak like they're talking to a kitten, or a child. They mean well."

He gets it—my comrade, my confidant, my teenage soulmate in the clan.

"You should tell them, 'Hey I'm still *me* in here.'" He turns the old photo of me all dolled-up toward me for proof.

Lately, Charlie's been constantly asking me for my memorabilia—personal letters to my husband before we were married, old wartime photos, recordings, especially of me singing. Asking what's your favorite this and that? So touching that he cares. I'd thought perhaps he was making a birthday scrapbook of some sort, but he'd returned all the photos and scraps that are the only remnants left of me. Is he worried I'm almost gone? It's just a bruised leg; just a normal fall. Well, and those numbers the doctor keeps rattling off, pursing his lips, shaking his know-it-all head, that keep this princess trapped here in this tower.

Charlie kisses my cheek, and I light up as he pulls a package from behind his back. I untie the bow and pull the techno gizmo from the box.

"What have we here?" An iPad kind of thing. I don't dare say what I'm thinking; I'm too old to learn this stuff. I admonish myself; you are what you think.

He grins, pushes aside his long swath of black hair that floats above the two buzzed sides of his head, like our unfinished lawn when my late husband used to stop mid-chore to eat his lunch. Charlie flips the Do Not Disturb sign on the door.

I tilt my head at that—what's on this thing that no one else should see? I'm intrigued.

He touches the button to turn it on, and a miniature image of me appears on-screen…Me. Well, my *used-to-be*.

"Your avatar, '*Eva Marie*,' I made her for you, Happy Birthday, Grandy Eva. Eighty-nine-years-young tomorrow."

That brings my smile and an unexpected ache in my chest. "Avatar?" It's a term that's vaguely familiar, some movie, some cartoon? There on the screen of the iPad floats a vision of myself on a carrier twittering a tune to smiling sailors. My face, my smile, my body, my hair coiffed forties-style, wearing a true-to-life sailor-girl suit—blouse and skirt, cinched tight—and our trio—those famous Back-up Babes and me.

My avatar, looks left, then right, tilts her head, so coy, awaiting my command. I can perfectly project the emotions I am feeling on her digitized face by a single tap; I click on the smile command and she smiles. I mean, *I* smile. I can perfectly *feel* the way she's looking, a bit sassy, a touch coquettish. The photos bring my memories to life. She has my habit of running fingers through her hair to show confusion or flirtation. She has *me* down to a T.

"See, I designed a replica of *you*. You can control her like this." Charlie runs through a series of touches and clicks on the screen. "It's from this new software. Like you can build a life. See?"

I get to know myself a little better, as I practice moving my avatar-self through some of the *digi-places*—the made-up word Charlie uses for the locations he's designed for me. It's as though I am actually walking down the streets. Realistic replicas of life.

"Watch this." Charlie, clicks and the American flags behind my yesteryear avatar blow in a westerly wind, and the setting sun threatens the need for spotlights on the carrier. Angled beams flash off the windows of the readied fighter planes. "Boogie Woogie Bugle Boy," a recording of the hit song comes on with my voice jump-jazzing the words. It makes me laugh out loud, cover my face and peek through my fingers, almost smelling the faint scent of fume and fragrance. We watch my avatar's lips move to the lyrics, her body to the sound, her hand wrapped around the giant old-time microphone. My own hand moist now with the memory.

"I gave you Paris, too. He swipes a finger across the screen."

"Aw, Charlie, so sweet, darling boy." I put the iPad beside me on the nightstand, pull his delighted head toward me, and kiss him. I'm thrilled. "So wonderful, Charlie, how did you ever?"

"Wait, that's not it. Look…" He clicks it alive again and watches me practice until the visiting hours end. "See you tomorrow, Grandy. Love you."

It isn't long before I am living my life out loud again, my songs, my scenes, my dreams, moving across the screen at will, running on the beach, singing—my voice linked from the old records to my avatar's lips. It's as though I can feel who I am again; be who I was again. The green walls of the rehab center that had sucked the joy from my days, fade into the background as I peruse the streets of Paris. My folds of flaccid muscles find their fortitude again on-screen.

When I tire of exploring Paris and all the charming Parisian men I see; tire of all the coffee and croissants my avatar can fearlessly eat—slathered in butter and fruits of the forest preserves; tire of sitting in a rickety wooden chair in a charming café near Montmartre; exhaust myself having my youthful sketch done by a charming man in a felt beret who gives me a double-cheek kiss goodbye—I learn to travel home across the screen to Delaware, to my *digi-summer home* in Rehoboth Beach.

After three days of non-stop time travel as my avatar, as my youthful *me*, I'm yet to interact with other avatars that I see. I'm too shy. Voyeur seems to be the very most I can muster. Charlie says I'll feel more at ease, somewhere where I feel at home.

This is the first year I can't make it to my beach house with my friends flowing in and out—a loss Charlie knows makes me ache inside. This damn leg, and something else I suspect. I'd been feeling weaker by the day, these past weeks. I'm grounded by a passing storm called aging that swept in without a warning and took me down.

"No need to be left out—I've created Rehoboth here," Charlie says, demonstrating how to stroll the board walk; negotiate the rides at Funland; sip steamy lattes at the Coffee Mill in my favorite bricked alley; flip my finger along the book titles at BrowseAbout book store for something new to read; and navigate the shoreline—all as my avatar.

"Such a smart boy; how did you ever think of this?" I ask during one of Charlie's many reminiscing visits.

"My friend made one for his grandfather, too. I thought it was so cool. You said *cool* back in the day, too, right, Grandy?"

Well, in one of my back-in-the-days, I'm sure I said, "cool." I'm delighted, grinning that he's created that beach world for me. For a week I enjoy the treats of being in my digitized existence in Rehoboth. I walk along the fantasy shore one morning after the nurse takes away the tan tray with my half-eaten breakfast. I'm anxious to get back to my life online. Jogging toward me is a handsome man about my avatar's age, well, maybe a bit older. He has a dog, a rusty colored solid-bodied brute, named Duke. I feel an electricity from days gone by. Am I cheating, if my husband's passed, and I flirt with a man, if I'm an avatar? Ridiculous. The intersection of my past and present causes a moment of confusion. Not eighty-nine *inside*, I think. I feel silly, but I grin and let myself have it, after all…it's not real. "Good morning." I smile.

"Hello," I get a smile back. His dog decides he likes me, puts his front legs down, and with derrière in air he wags his tail as though he knows me. "That's funny, he never does that with anyone else." The man stands alert, so the dog doesn't jump up on me. A gentleman.

There's a moment, a flirtation of the eyes. My avatar, Eva Marie—I guess it's me—actually reddens—a blood-rushing blush.

I affix my glasses straighter on my aging face, shift in my chair, pause the scene on the iPad, and hobble up to open the hospital room window. I need a gulp of that fresh early summer air. Feeling a tad flushed. I get my composure, and quickly click back on.

"Shall we walk together…as long as we're both here?" the realistic robot says.

It seems there is no point in playing hard to get, one can be so bold and free when playing games. If it ever gets to be too much, so easy to just shut down the screen. I want to maintain my manners and mores with the arresting stranger, but I'm out of my element here, so I say, *yes*. I'm glad not to be constrained by the times, any times—past or present. Smiling down at my swollen propped-up leg that is invisible to my avatar admirer, I turn away from the dresser mirror. Why ruin my own illusion?

His name is David. David Lakefield. In just a few circumspect glances, I notice his muscled shoulders, lean waist, a body I can picture swooping out of a pool, chestnut hair flipping a spiral of droplets after a deliberate fifty-two laps. A Burt Lancaster kind of guy.

We share stories, have so much in common, seem to know each other from the start. Standing at Dolle's Salt water taffy stand, we fill our box with the same favorites.

"I bet you like licorice." He winks. "So, do I. Well, now I do."

Among one hundred flavors of ice cream, we both order Jamoca Almond Fudge. We can hold each other's gaze more easily knowing it's pretend; or is it? It sends a tingle down my arms. So real, the feelings, as real as I've ever felt.

He tells me of the books he's read; I've read them, too. Then we chat about our favorite movies with a familiarity I've missed. We're the same age. Our conversations are so satisfying, we're on point politically—progressive. He complains about discrimination. Says his son's married, and gay. David has one grandson, Jonathon, loves him. They're very close.

I agree, and agree, and agree, as subject after subject unravels who we are. David was in theatre, played my favorite Shakespeare roles. When he hears that I'm a former singer, he quotes, *"If music be the food of love, play on."*

Romantic, like me. Good. I feel the rosie-red of my face, remembering a long-ago memory, somehow my body can't forget. When I first met my late husband, crossing the room to stand before me at the USO dance at the top of a Boston hotel ballroom—the heat in my face, and the allure of his smile.

I click off the screen, feeling awkward. Try to wait, then turn it on again.

I huddle in my room each day, irritated by the interruptions—the nurse, meds, blood pressure. Oh, dear God that awful rehab, lifting little rubber-coated weights with weakened arms when I could be back with my buff boy eating calorie-free Grotto's pizza with abandon. I can't wait to get back to being me, on my screen, with David, in my preferred life.

Sitting in the lounge chair by the window with my iPad, the sun on my shoulder, the breeze in my hair, makes time on the beach with David feel even more alive. On the seventh day since I've arrived in digi-Rehoboth, David spots a pod of dolphins. Such a thrill.

He puts his hand on my shoulder to point them out, squeezes, and a charge goes down my arm. "See? Eleven o'clock?" he says, leans his head in next to mine, and speaks into my hair.

I tremble. Oh yes, I *see* them! Two dolphins simultaneously leap into the air, and splash down at twelve. We're moving forward, too. I feel the warmth of our friendship, the beginning of a romance. Dear Lord, I'm an old woman, for Pete's sake. I laugh but let myself go on. I'm not dead yet.

My eyes follow his muscled arm as it surrounds me and pulls me in for our first real kiss that feels like a replay, like it's happened a thousand times before. His shiny hair lights up in the afternoon shafts of sunlight that stripe the beach with shadow as the glowing orb drops behind the town. His blue eyes are the kind that change with the light, like the cerulean sea behind us. I stand facing him, the ocean roars in a rhythm, crashes in a cadence that seems to mimic the pounding of my heart.

My resurrection begins to lift my vitals, lowers my blood pressure, heals all the things my medical reports can measure.

"I'm impressed. Your EKG looks good," my doctor says.

Ha! He doesn't hear the flutters and skips on any EKG when I'm online with David, and I say nothing of my travels against his orders as my invincible avatar, Eva Marie. The *real* me.

"I'm releasing you to go home, Mrs. Andrews."

Go home? I never thought I'd hear the words.

"It's a near miracle," he says.

I smile. "Yes, it is."

My daughter picks me up from rehab and drives me to my beach house for the summer. I haven't told her about my favorite pastime. I feel guilty as though I'm having a secret love affair. And then, I'm truly in my Rehoboth home, filled with sweet memories like a full candy jar, but absent of my David. My daughter fusses over me. So sweet, but I need some privacy.

Charlie arrives that evening. I'm sitting on the porch in one of our rockers, and he joins me. The shade has taken over the painted planks on my covered porch, one of those extra salty, balmy June nights in store.

"How's it been going?"

"My health's taken a good turn, the doctor says—"

"So glad to get you out of that place. You look great. But, uh…how about *online?* I mean, you had the guts to meet someone yet?"

I tell him the truth; he's the only one who deserves it. He has a funny look on his face. No one puts much over on this Grandy. "What are you up to, Charlie?"

"Nothing, it's just cool, right? He runs his fingers through the hedge on top of his head. Can we hit the boardwalk tomorrow afternoon? You up to it?"

"Of course, but a short walk, sweetheart, OK?" That's my doctor talking, I think. I've been tread-milling twice a day since the cast came off. I feel *well*…no, I feel amazing.

As I dress in the morning, I wonder what will it be like to be at the beach without my David? Wait, there is no *my David*. I laugh, and for the first time I dare to think about the person on the other side of my avatar romance. Is it some pimply, teenage boy? Goodness, I never thought of that before. Why didn't I think of that? A young technology nerd in Thailand? Adolescent in Africa? Lonely old man in Oklahoma? My partner's on another planet as far as I know. That thought deflates me. No matter, the emotions were real, the experience so wonderful, and now I'm well enough to be right where I want to be, I tell myself. My beloved beach town. Well worth it.

After lunch I send a message to David; I tell him, *TTYL,* as I sign off. *Talk to you later,* one of many short-hand phrases, the internet acronyms Charlie has taught me. I add, *I'll miss you.* OMG, I'm in too deep; I have no idea what I'm doing with this techy stuff. Am I tech-addicted, like my daughter says Charlie is?

I hear my daughter coming into the room; I pretend to be asleep. She takes my gizmo from my lap and sets it on the table and kisses me on my forehead. I feel the invasion; I hold my breath; feel the loss; I pray David doesn't answer me just yet. She leaves. I exhale.

No answer from David for a few minutes. I can't help curling in my shoulders, arms holding myself, grinning like a young girl when the bird-whistle signals the arrival of his return message. David answers, *Me too. Later. Missing you.* I choose to not imagine who my David really is;

he's who I think he is. Really, isn't that the point? Like the imaginary friend my daughter had at three years old. Why destroy the dream?

Charlie drives to Rehoboth Avenue, drops me by the bandstand, and looks for parking. "Why did you bring your laptop," I ask?

"Uh…I'm meeting a friend to play a game. Here he comes, now."

He introduces his friend, Jay, sweet blonde with an Oriole's baseball cap on backwards, and they plop on a white bench in front of Candy Kitchen and begin to click away.

"Grandy, you gotta feel the sand, take a walk by the water. Need my help?"

"I'm fine." I haven't walked on sand for so long. My feet have only fast-forwarded on a treadmill these past weeks. I take my shoes off. Bending isn't easy, but I have more energy than I've had in years. I make it to the edge of the water. The cool wet sand's so soothing. It's almost as if the gulls remember me. They swoop down to greet me. The ocean curls just right and foam pursues me and hisses over my feet.

Only one man is on the beach wearing shorts and a Harvard hoodie. He whistles to a dog who's out of sight behind the dunes. The ruddy dog sidetracks and rushes toward me, curious, twisting left and right, bounding in a way that isn't threatening.

"Duke?" The man calls the dog.

Did I hear right? *Duke?* I'm confused. I hear my name, "Graaaandy!" I look over my shoulder and Charlie and Jay are standing on the bench pointing toward the man, cheering, hooting, high-fiving each other.

The man approaches, silver-haired, walking with the drag of feet that have marched many years, like mine.

The dog is at my feet, derriere in air, tail wagging. Making little whimpering sounds.

The familiar man comes closer with his handsome head tilted. This is no avatar; this is real, happening IRL.

"*Eva Marie?*"

I can see the resemblance blurred by many years, but there he stands, blue-eyed before me. "*David?*"

"It appears we have been had by modern-day matchmakers," he says pointing back at the boys.

"Modern-day, what? Oh, my." I laugh as it sinks in. "So, that's why Charlie has been collecting my memorabilia."

"And this is the project my grandson, Jonathan was working on so diligently, interviewing me about my past."

"And Charlie's buddy is your grandson Jonathan—Jay." My dim light is finally glowing; I get it. They used some special software to make me come alive, make *us* come alive.

David shifts the leash around his leg. "Thank goodness you're mature and beautiful. I imagine that unripe lovely avatar would be quite disappointed by my current seasoned-self in the flesh."

Plucking the word *beautiful* from his sentence, my heart races. Not the kind of flutter that worries me, but the kind I haven't felt in quite a while. I'm happy to resurrect that feeling. There's a clear attraction to this lovely man. I'm happy that I have kept myself in good shape—well, not bad for nearly ninety, and I've been living through my avatar for weeks. I laugh inside at my remnant of foolish vanity and distract myself by ruffling the dog's head.

"Look. One o'clock." He extends his arm with pointed finger over my shoulder, tucks in behind me, leans his cheek against mine and whispers, "See them?" I hold my breath. Their slick and leathered backs rise up, arch, and stitch their way through the sea, in shadow against the orange and gold horizon.

Is it silly to use the word *swoon* at this age, in these times? No way to shut down the screen on this scene; no need. I'm glad not to be constrained by the times, any times, before or now. It seems there is no point in playing hard to get.

David reaches out his weathered hand and takes mine. I am comfortable with his thickened veins, like tree roots weaving in and out of a welcoming wooded trail. The applause and howls of our grandsons rise behind us, and we release a blended laugh in harmony. The squeeze of his hand is asking me to stay. Where is this path going? I'm too wise to ask, too old to care. That's a question for a former, cautious me with something left to lose. So much to gain, a reason for me to greet each day now that all my friends have passed on. Someone to see beyond my wrinkled packaging to the woman alive inside.

I imagine us walking together on the beach each day. Hosting barbeques with new friends. I feel his body seated beside me on the piano bench. I hear his laugh when I knock his blue Bocce ball away from the silver pallino ball, stealing his points away. I imagine our good-hearted arguments over a book we've both read. "I feel as though we've truly had a past, well, an iPad-past."

"It's surreal, huh?" He lifts his elbow toward me.

I tuck my arm in his. "So, is this our present or our future?"

His deep laugh is wrapped in velvet. "And yet we've just met and have so much to learn." He finishes my thought, and drops his eyes to the sand, bends, picks up a battered shell, the tiny, fragile see-through caramel-colored kind, and closes it in my palm. "Shall we walk together, as long as we're both here in our 'now'?"

Morning sun lights his still-handsome, craggy, aging face, and his straightened shoulders lift in a hopeful plea.

My used-to-be, my *real me*...we say, yes.

Why She Never Asked Why

He didn't *get a PhD to stay home
with a baby* she felt a burn in her gut
but she didn't complain this was
the life she'd always wanted
a husband a degree a teaching job happy
to take his name his friends his hobbies
happy to shoot a gun bait a hook
portage into the wilderness
instead of concerts and plays happy
to postpone her Masters while he got his
happy to follow him to grad school to
anti-war protests to Canada
if he got drafted

She noticed the *girls* in the movement
made the coffee typed the letters
nursed the babies walked
behind the men who made speeches
spoke to the media led the marches so
she read Gloria Steinem devoured
Simone de Beauvoir started to ask why
men have better jobs more money
raising her daughter she wondered
why girls didn't play baseball basketball
take chemistry or trig didn't expect to be
doctors or engineers why she could only
nurse type or teach her principal asked
*who will care for your baby when she's
sick* the school psychologist asked *aren't
you afraid you'll ruin your child* she asked
why no one ever asked the baby's dad and
why she never asked why

She moved out she petitioned protested
rallied for rights fought for joint custody
after the lawyer said *children belong with
the mother* she bought a house of her own
trucks garden tools and a lop-eared rabbit
for her daughter brought her to rallies
marches meetings concerts and plays
winter vacations she couldn't afford

She got a new job made women friends
joined a soccer team learned
she could sweat ran a 5K a 10K a
marathon and many more kept running
carried the torch for thirty years she
doesn't protest any more but mention *the
glass ceiling*
80 cents to the man's dollar
or call her *girl*
like a match to tinder
her spark ignites and burns
in the daughter
who won't march in the street
brew the men's coffee
or live the lie

Sherri Wright

Lost and Found Again

I had given up hope of ever finding her letter

Stephanie Fowler

My wife, Patty, and I pulled up to the storage unit as the August sun burned orange in the late afternoon sky. We found my mom's unit and put the windows down in the back seat for Lima. She stuck her head out and barked at a squirrel nonchalantly hopping around on the other side of the chain-link fence.

"18–3–21," I called to Patty. The padlock stuck a little but gave way, and the metal door groaned and screeched as we slung it upwards. The smell of cardboard boxes and the faintest whiff of mildew greeted us. It was a familiar smell, like the stale air in your grandma's attic or the metallic aftertaste of your father's garage. It was the smell of memories, all covered in cobwebs and dust and too much darkness.

In total, there were about a dozen boxes plus old computers, a coat rack from my childhood bedroom, and two lime green chaise lounge chairs. These were not mine; I was sure of it, but my job was not to pick and choose. My job was to get it all out.

"All this has to go?" Patty asked, one eyebrow slightly curved upward.

"Yeah. We're leaving nothing behind but the mouse turds." I pushed aside a cardboard lid on the box closest to the door and surveyed the contents. Junior high yearbooks, a term paper from college on Wallace Thurman's, *The Blacker the Berry*, an old diary, stacks of mismatched photographs, a sticker book from elementary school. Things I'd once loved or deemed worth saving, and yet forgot anyway.

As I rifled through the box, I paused over a few photographs. One was a black and white photo strip. My high school sweetheart used to take me on dates to the Ocean City boardwalk and we'd jump into those old photo booths every time we went. *We were so young*, I thought. *We were just babies—both of us all chubby cheeks and bright eyes.* I smiled as I thought about riding around in his beat up, late 80s Honda Civic.

Another photo caught my attention. It was grainy and wrinkled in one corner. Taken on our porch, my first dog, Bridgette, was sprawled out on a white whicker sofa. She was a Norwegian Elkhound. I was four-years-old when we got her, back in 1983. I have no idea where the name came from, but she was beautiful. *God, I hadn't thought about that dog in years.* Loved the cold weather. Never wanted to come inside. Once during a terrible storm, my mom had brought her in the house. She'd panted and paced and finally sat down at the back door, staring intently at it as though willing it to open.

I saw pictures of my childhood home. My mother's decor in the '90s was country: dark plaids, floral wallpaper, Longaberger baskets, dried potpourri, hearts and angels and wreaths. Our house always smelled like cinnamon and sugar cookies or wild berries and rose hips. But in her defense, I feel like almost every suburban house in my town looked and smelled exactly like this.

Somewhere near the bottom of the box, my fingers brushed a small envelope and my heart leapt. *Her letter! How did it get here, though, mixed in with the stuff of my childhood bedroom? And why hadn't I thought to look here before now?* My head was dizzy with excitement … Countless times I had ripped through my garage and attic and old books and my hope chest and anywhere else I could think, but finally I resigned myself to its "forever" loss, angry and frustrated that I hadn't been more careful with something so precious. Finding it again was pure elation and relief. And heartbreak.

Alice Davis was my high school English teacher. I loved her. During my senior year, I had a rough time, and she was the only person who noticed I was struggling. My mother was going into renal failure after a severe allergic reaction and the local doctors seemed completely unable to help her or stop the damage. An acute sense of terror grew within me. I was afraid of losing her. I tried to keep a brave face at home for my mom and for my sister. But my stupid tender heart broke one day at school. It broke in front of Alice Davis.

I remember crying in her arms as I blubbered on about how my mom was so sick, how I was scared of losing her, how I was getting ready to go to college and I didn't think I could make it without her, and how I worried about my little sister and what life was going to be like for her… and on and on and on. Alice hugged me. She'd let me get it all out. All the fear and doubt and anger—every bit of the poison. From then on, she took me under her wing and mentored me through it.

But in her classroom, I had to work. Just because she understood what I was going through did not give me a pass. No, no. I might have been going through a difficult time, but work was necessary and there was no such thing as a valid excuse or a reason to quit. There was no use in feeling sorry for myself. In this she taught me a lesson: work through the heartache ... *work because of the heartache.*

Although straight-laced and reserved, she encouraged the writing non-conformist in me, even when my essays went against her natural grain. Once I wrote a paper on the legalization of marijuana for her class. That one made her eyes roll, but as always, she judged me on the merits of my work and ability, not the content of my irreverent high school essays.

Alice Davis got me through my senior year of high school. That is not hyperbole.

In the light of a setting August sun, I opened the little envelope. Inside, on a notecard emblazed with the Parkside High School crest, she wrote in blue ink and lovely cursive. The date was April 21, 2006.

> *Dear Stephanie,*
> *I know this thank you note is ridiculously late, but I do want you to know how much we all appreciated you taking the time to come in and speak at the Straight A reception. They really needed to hear what you had to say, and it was obvious that everyone enjoyed your remarks. On a personal note, it was so good to see you and to find out how you have been and what you're doing. Thanks again and take care. You are very special and talented, and I know you will continue to do well in the future.*
> *Sincerely,*
> *Alice Davis*

This was it. This was the last thing she ever said to me. Five and a half years after she wrote this note, Alice Davis was gone. Murdered by her husband. Brutally so.

I read the note again and wept.

Writing had always been my pathway to understanding. Only through these messy words on the page could I come to terms with the ramblings of my mind and the experiences of my life. Ink scrawlings on paper and in journals: this is how I make my peace. I know no other way.

When Alice was murdered, I knew one day I would write about it. About her. No one could make sense of what happened. Those who knew her could not reconcile this gentle soul with the horrific violence inflicted upon her. In the days that followed, news reports recounted the strange and awful details of her death and her life. We were left mouths agape, devastated and dumbstruck. And for me, the only way I figured I would be able to make any sort of peace with it would be to write.

In June 2015, I decided it was time and I was off to a furious start: interviews, Freedom of Information Act filings for police reports, autopsy and toxicology reports, and newspaper archives. By the end of the year, however, I had hit a roadblock. The story wasn't coming together correctly. Something was off. I was losing patience and growing frustrated. I'd begun to sink into clichés: bitten off more than I could chew, in water over my head, not up to snuff...

Then I had a wedding to plan, and not long after the wedding, my wife and I were in a terrible accident which sent her to the Shock Trauma Unit and later required facial reconstruction surgery and a lengthy recovery from a traumatic brain injury. Between my overwhelming writer's block and recovery from the accident, Alice's story went cold. I was exhausted and empty, and a story like this one, complex and emotional, needed more of me than I had to give. So, as much as it bothered me, I let the story sit for about a year and a half, collecting dust in a file box next to my desk ... a writing desk belonging to a writer who wasn't writing much of anything good at all. I grew angry with myself and I tried to fight back feelings of failure and resentment but finding little relief. I was stuck in *that*.

Until I found something I had lost.

The letter from Alice.

Before you start thinking it was a simple solution or tidy happy-ever-after-ending, let me help you check that notion right now. Writing is anything but easy; writing is a delicious agony. Anyone who ever thinks, "Oh, I can write a book! There's nothing to it!" is either positively delusional or profoundly unaware of the rigors and mental endurance required if one seeks to do it well.

Often, it is hell on earth followed by glimpses of an Eden one can only witness from the outside. But those glimpses, though... oh, they are enough.

I took Alice's letter and tucked it inside an old copy of *The Fourth Edition of Literature: Structure, Sound, and Sense* by Laurence Perrine. At the end of the school year, as I had prepared to go off to college, I'd asked Alice if she had any extra copies. We had used it as a textbook. She had smiled at me and dug through a stack of books. She found one: the cover was torn in several places and was held together by copious amounts of masking tape. I had written my name and year 1997 in pencil on its inside cover. I'd also wrote: "on loan from Mrs. Davis," as though I had the intention of giving it back.

Just after Christmas Day 2017, I sat down at my writing desk and resolved to finish what I'd started. Perhaps it was the excruciating thought of facing down another year with her story left undone. I lifted the lid on the file box and started again. My fingers have been on the keyboard every day, my pen on the paper. My mind is singularly focused in a way that feels old and familiar to me.

I wish I could say every sentence is spectacular, and I'm a writer moving through moments of genius. Untrue. I come to the page daily, eager to start and loathe to stop. Her story is now a bonfire in my belly and I am no longer afraid of it. Writing, I have remembered now, is muscle memory and so I sit in this chair and I do the damned work. After all, there are no revisions which can be made to an empty page.

So here I am.

Because one must work through the heartaches.

Tadasana—Mountain Pose

In the studio, it is easy
to imagine myself
a mountain.
Standing on carpet, looking
out the window
at the benevolent tree
in the parking lot
that whispers its leaves
against the glass,
I can be anything I wish:
tree, moon, mountain.

But some days, feet stumbling
on forest path or sidewalk, face
burned by real wind,
it takes more than imagination
to believe myself
a granite edifice carved
by centuries of rain.

Then, hand on heart,
it is a supreme act of will
that keeps my legs steady,
that lifts the crown of my head
to a gray swollen sky
and dares the earth
to not crumble beneath me.

Ellen Collins

Originally published in Ellen's book, *Invitations: Poems of Yoga and Meditation* in 2017

Vrksasana—Tree Pose

In winter we see the true design of a tree,
how the branches are its bones,
and life pulses deep beneath that ragged bark
even though it appears
that it is only a brittle replica of its summer self.
Cold rain and an avalanche of heavy snow, winds
that race down the mountain,
a thin transparent sun at noon.
All this the tree knows.

It has learned, in its wisdom,
how to bend, how to hold, how
to go deep within where in autumn
it stored huge swallows of orange light.
It has learned
how to wait and trust, to believe
it can stand still without falling.

On my blue mat,
I wonder if my roots can ground me,
if I can be straight, if I can breathe
through my fear that I will fall.
I think about that tree outside my bedroom window,
how it holds its arms out for the winter wrens,
how it shudders in gusts
but returns upright again.
I know if I am to stand,
if I am to lift one foot and let
the other hold me up,

I must have the faith of a tree,
and the generosity
to lift my hands for whatever
winged being might want
to land
there.

Ellen Collins

Originally published in Ellen's book, *Invitations: Poems of Yoga and Meditation* in 2017.

Logjam

Mimi S Dupont

I am a walking logjam.

Logjam [lawg-jam] Noun. An immovable pileup or tangle of logs, as in a river, causing a blockage; any blockage or massive accumulation.

An immovable pileup. The emotional baggage of all these years I've piled up into my lifetime is clogging my arteries like plaque, damming up my vital organs like drowned tree trunks wedged between rocks as an angry river rages downstream in a deluge. Anger was something we didn't do, didn't feel, didn't deal with during my childhood. Anger was something unacceptable because … well, no one ever said *why* because our family didn't *talk* about being angry either. But I think we didn't talk about anger, didn't express anger, didn't even acknowledge we felt anger because anger is an emotion, and we didn't do much of that illogical, irrational, unreasonable stuff. We pretended emotions were nearly nonexistent. Ours and everyone else's. An inconvenient but incontrovertible part of our cerebral selves being forced to occupy a body like a prisoner of war occupies a cage. We would no more discuss emotions than we would describe having sex or the content of our bowel movements. Sure, we could be excited about a birthday, pleased with a Christmas present, disappointed that the cookie jar was empty. But anger was not just an emotion, it was a *strong* emotion. Feeling anger might cause dangerous, erratic, possibly even violent behavior. One might get carried away. Behave badly. Lose control. One might lose a crucial relationship. Lose someone's love. Be abandoned. So we kept all those pesky emotions bottled up with a very tight stopper. I'm pretty sure I have an immovable pileup at multiple locations – in my larynx from all the swallowed words, in my heart from hurts real and imagined, in my stomach from my mother's sometimes acidic comments. Each pileup is jammed into place with

A tangle of logs. Each bit of my emotional baggage is another log, another snapped off tree trunk, its bark raked by the ragged rocks against which it has beaten itself, if only briefly, pressed on feverishly by a river running wild. The words pile up somewhere inside me, compacted, under constant pressure, just as trees with torn limbs bent away at alarming angles from the trunk pile up one by one, each wedging itself into the collected mass of downed dogwoods and redbud, ashes and oaks rising higher and higher like a rebel stronghold's makeshift wall or floating flotsam trapping a runaway kayak taking its terrified paddler careening toward a precipice

As in a river. A dammed river. Provided they are fed, rivers flow. When spring brings the snowmelt or rain falls for days at a time, a swollen river can race down any incline taking everything movable in its path. Whole trees are wrenched by their roots from previously safe perches on riverbanks and dragged downstream in the rush of the rapids

Causing a blockage. Are the arteries of my writing heart sixty percent blocked? Eighty percent? Are all of my arteries blocked? Only some? I must move this

Massive accumulation. Must move this lifetime of unexpressed irritation, anger, frustration, rage I did not know was holed up inside me until it began to ooze up and out of my personal volcano. But I can feel it now —choking me, smothering me, cutting off the air I need to breathe, clogging the veins that feed my writing heart. What I need is

Release [ri-lees] Verb. To free from confinement, bondage, obligation, pain; to give up, relinquish, surrender.

When the logjam breaks free, the raging water will push the sodden mass to the sides and continue racing savagely toward its end. Forests will be ravaged. Farms will be flooded. Bridges will burst from their foundations and roads will cave in.

What will my larynx be like when the dammed-up words burst forth? Will my throat hurt? Will my voice be hoarse? Will I ever speak normally again?

What will my heart be like when the hurts are released, the perpetrators named, faced and hopefully forgiven? Will the blood flow freely through my veins enlivening every extremity?

What will my stomach be like when the acid is neutralized? Will it greet whatever I eat with equanimity and do its job without the drama?

This essay is finished. But I am just beginning. I am still a walking logjam.

Poem for Henry

Earth teach me stillness
as the grasses are stilled with light.
Earth teach me suffering
as old stones suffer with memory.
Earth teach me humility
as blossoms are humble with beginning.
Earth teach me caring
as the mother who secures her young.
Earth teach me courage
as the tree which stands alone.
Earth teach me limitation
as the ant who crawls on the ground.
Earth teach me freedom
as the eagle which soars in the sky.
Earth teach me resignation
as the leaves which die in the fall.
Earth teach me regeneration
as the seed which rises in the spring.
Earth teach me to forget myself
as melted snow forgets its life.
Earth teach me to remember kindness
as dry fields weep with rain.

Jane Bender (April 18, 2016)

Published posthumously for Jane O'Rourke Bender, August 4, 1946-September 25, 2016.

She writes because
        her sisters are hurting
because she has no other way
        to comfort them
               but with her words

Columbus Day

Sarah Barnett

If you happened to pass the three-story Victorian house, you might think it was a bed-and-breakfast. You wouldn't see anyone relaxing on the wraparound front porch, though. In 1959 if you were unmarried and pregnant, you needed to hide. Your parents made up a story—trying out another school, tending to a sick relative. Really you were at the Shoreview Home for Unmarried Mothers across the street from the Saint Somebody-or-Other Catholic School for Girls, discreetly located in a forgettable New Jersey beach town. No boardwalk or hotels meant no tourists and little chance of running into acquaintances.

Only Brenda and Sy, volunteer dance teachers, treated us like normal kids. They waltzed in on Saturday night with their records, and for a couple of hours we did the lindy and the cha-cha in the living room, the sagging sofas pushed against the wall.

We were learning a Japanese folk dance, pretending to be workers harvesting rice, when Ellen sank to the floor. She was only five months pregnant. A social worker took her to the hospital. Next day they told us the baby had stopped growing and died inside her.

The first thought I had was, "Lucky." Didn't the others think Ellen was lucky too? If some fairy godmother had fluttered out of a storybook and granted each of us one wish, wouldn't we imagine returning to a time when we were never pregnant? Weren't we going to pretend exactly that when we went home?

Ellen wouldn't have to pretend. She could go back to high school and the rest of her life.

Now, over 50 years later, I think I've learned something about luck. And I still wonder if any of it would have happened if we hadn't gone to the beach that day.

Ellen, Laurie and I were sent to the dentist in a taxi. It was Columbus Day, and when we left the office people were walking around enjoying their day off and the unseasonably warm weather. The pizza place next to the dentist had a holiday special—three sizes of round pans labeled "Nina," "Pinta," and "Santa Maria." Girls our age were hanging around

Woolworths and getting ice cream cones from the candy store. "I can't go back yet," I said.

"Whaddya mean?" Laurie said.

"Let's go sit on the beach. Nobody'll know how long the dentist took."

"We'll get in trouble," Ellen said.

"What can they do?" I started walking down the main street toward the beach. Glancing back, I was almost surprised to see Ellen and Laurie following. Our maternity tops floated over our straight skirts as we walked. We pretended to ignore the looks we got from bystanders, equal parts curiosity and contempt. We wore the required wedding rings. As if gold bands would keep people from noticing that we were barely out of the hopscotch stage.

I couldn't help checking my reflection in the store windows we passed. Was I still hoping that the short girl with the dark pony tail and the huge stomach wasn't me? Would I ever get used to the idea that an actual baby was inside?

As we neared the beach, a gust of wind blew Laurie's pleated top up to her face. "God," she said, as she smoothed it back over her belly, "I feel as big as a boat."

Laurie wore hoop earrings the size of yo-yos, brilliant blue eye shadow, and her streaked blonde hair added three inches to her height. She had turned up the collar of her blue maternity top, a style my mother would have termed "trashy." On her feet she wore flip-flops, the rubber kind you bought at bargain stores three pair for a dollar. Next to her Ellen and I looked mousey. We hadn't bothered with make-up. "Nice girl" brown leather loafers covered our feet.

At Shoreview most of the girls steered clear of Laurie, but I wanted to know her better. I couldn't help wondering how someone who seemed so tough and smart had gotten herself pregnant like the rest of us.

We made our way to a space near the water. It was low tide. The waves had carved a hill out of the sand with a shelf at the top where I flopped down and slipped off my shoes. Before us was a scene from a coloring book—blue sky, sparkling ocean, large boat floating near the horizon. Families sat on the sand in groups, small solar systems with children orbiting adults. A setting so achingly normal, I felt like laughing and crying at the same time.

"Ellen, take off your shoes." She ignored me, sitting stiffly while twisting the gold wedding band on her swollen finger. Laurie walked along the shore picking up stones and skipping them across the water. I admired her sidearm throw, something boys usually did better than girls.

"We should head back," Ellen said.

"Relax. It'll be fine."

Laurie came to sit with us and leaned back to get the sun on her face. Ellen removed her shoes, dropping her wedding band into one of them. Her dark curly hair had started to frizz in the humidity.

A family sat nearby—mom, dad and three girls. Mom and the two older kids, who looked about six and eight, were scooping sand into a large pile. The baby, who had strawberry blonde hair like her mom, must have just learned to walk. Dad had rolled up the sleeves of his dress shirt and stood at the bottom of the hill as the toddler rushed toward his open arms. He scooped her up and planted her back at the top of the hill. "Up you go, Josie," he said, and rushed back to the bottom in his bare feet.

They repeated the game over and over, she giggling and shrieking, teetering from side to side, almost out of control, the sash of her pink dress trailing behind her. Eventually, Josie refused help, making her way to the top alone, digging chubby legs into the sand, staggering a little, putting one hand down for balance as she climbed. Then she waddled down the hill while sagging rubber pants slipped almost to her knees. Dad reached over, trying to fix them, but she was already moving up. Again, she raced down the hill, gathering speed, not able to stop. He blocked her just as she was about to get wet, tried to pick her up, but she shook him off with a babble of scolding that needed no translation.

We watched this scene as if it were a movie. I turned away after a while to watch the ocean, picturing myself floating, my body losing its clumsiness. When I was younger I would stand at the shoreline and imagine swimming to Europe. The ocean evoked a world of possibilities, all the places grownups could go. But from where I sat, it seemed entirely possible to sail far enough to fall off the edge.

When I looked again the family had started to pack up. The older sisters stomped out the castle they'd constructed, while the parents stretched their blanket between them and folded it, first in half lengthwise, then walked toward each other bringing the ends together. They didn't notice that Josie had wandered close to where the waves broke. She waved her arms while her feet did a splash dance in the receding water.

Three of us must have had the same thought at the same time. I shuffled clumsily down the hill, reaching Josie just as she was thrown off balance by an incoming wave. She shrieked, as water surged over her legs and waist. I grabbed at her hand, but she screamed and resisted with surprising strength. I should have bent down and picked her up, but my stomach was in the way. I was pulling her to her feet when I turned around and saw Ellen sitting halfway down the hill. Laurie was helping her up.

The parents had come rushing over. Josie's mom took her daughter's hand from mine. "I think she's just scared," I said. The mom looked down at my stomach, then her eyes arrived somewhere in the neighborhood of mine, and she gave me half a smile. Dad came up and said, "Good grab. Thanks. Is your friend okay?"

Ellen was on her feet brushing sand from the back of her skirt. "I just slipped. I'm fine," she said.

"She's all right," Laurie said.

Dad picked up Josie, called to the other kids and they left after one more "thanks" and a "sure you're okay?"

The cab ride back was quiet. I didn't know what the others were thinking. I had spent the last few months trying not to think, switching off the part of my brain that looked to the future. I was replaying the family scene on the beach. Then I put the memory away, the way I sometimes squirreled away an extra cookie or two from dinner.

Getting back was easy as I'd promised. We wandered into Shoreview's living room where girls sat in groups, knitting, playing gin rummy, reading, and we acted like we'd never been gone.

At dinner, Ellen and I exchanged small smiles. But when I looked over at Laurie's table I saw the fight start. Later I learned that Jill had said something to Laurie about her shoes. *What's with the flip-flops? Didn't she know summer was over?*

"Snotty bitch," Laurie said. Then Jill said something, and Laurie flung a glass of milk. Most of it missed Jill and landed on the floor, but that was it. The "wardens" stepped in, walked Laurie away to a small office where phone calls were made. Then she was gone.

Ellen left a few days later. Even though I thought she had lucked out in some way, I tried not to wonder if she lost the baby because of the fall on the beach. I couldn't ask anyone, but I kept telling myself that pregnant women slipped every day and went on to have perfectly fine babies.

I never go to the beach without remembering that October day, imagining the three of us sitting on the sand, hands folded over bulging bellies. Could I have looked out to the horizon and seen the changing climate?

Ten years was all it took. After I left my infant daughter at Shoreview, after I had thrown my wedding ring into a restless ocean. Ten years later, young people were skinny dipping and dancing naked at Woodstock. Soon, single pregnant women had choices beyond signing adoption papers and pretending nothing had happened. The need to hide vanished along with the fashion for voluminous maternity clothes. The term "single mom" would become fashionable. Shoreview, renamed "Willow Academy," reinvented itself as a school for learning-disabled boys. There was even a reality TV show about young women who were *Sixteen and Pregnant*.

I was wrong about so many things.

I thought any hope for a real life was gone. I thought I would never marry, never have a family of my own.

I was wrong about Ellen. She wasn't the lucky one. Her baby would never run into a parent's waiting arms.

Lucky me. You weren't supposed to make friends at Shoreview. But Laurie managed to call me from her new "home," and we started a conversation that is still going strong.

Lucky them. Josie and her family. Once in a while when they're together, someone will say, "Remember that day Josie kept running up and down the hill at the beach?"

Lucky Columbus. He found something he wasn't even looking for.

Girls on the Street

Half past three on the stroll in Northwest
it's a slow night—and cold in spike heels and skirts
that barely cover our asses
too cold for the johns
to leave their warm homes in the suburbs

The white van is here
pushing the same damn brochures for
hotlines, counselors, social services
we take their free condoms but
what we need on a cold night
like this is hot coffee and bail
money if the cops run a sting

and tomorrow we'll need help
getting our kids into school
when they don't have
a permanent address except for
the shabby hotel on New York Avenue
where the pimp babysits and threatens
to take them away if we don't
bring him our money early in the morning

Look at the white bitch in the van tonight
with her tight smile and tailored suit
she's from the board of directors
and she wants to help us
get off the streets
get a GED
decent clothes
a real job
a proper home for our kids she says
we should start a new life

Doesn't she know
we've already started new lives
only now we make money
when we lay down for the men

Sherri Wright

Dancing with Strangers

Marjorie F. Weber

Over the years, I have been at least once to every singles venue, every bar within 20 miles of my home.

I have gone to singles mixers at VFW halls, the Basking Ridge Country Club, the old Mill Inn, the Unitarian Church, the Parsippany Hilton and the What's-Its-Name Restaurant in Bridgewater that I liked best with their summer patio dances outside in the evening air.

I have spent happy hours Friday evenings in low lit beery bars with names like Freddie's and Chatfield's, The Office, The Store and the Tewksbury Inn where we waltzed and cha cha-ed and boogied, line danced, and free-styled with men with blurred faces to the thump of tunes crooned by Stevie Wonder and Donna Summer, Michael Jackson and Elton John. Sometimes, in the dregs of the evening when the last dance was danced, and the lights went up, a man asked for my number or he gave me his card and we promised to meet. Sometimes we did.

In the beginning, I thought it would be temporary, this Friday night trolling, something all single people had to do, but not for long. I was still young, thirty-something, fresh off a divorce, new at this, my daughter just four. Surely, I'd meet someone soon.

Bleary-eyed after too long a day at work, I'd join my friends Denise or Nancy or Diane on a Friday night, all of us hoping that this stretch between married and single and married again, would be brief, that we would soon be back to the lovely humdrum of waking up with the same man every morning, sharing leftovers for dinner and Saturday night barbecues and Sunday morning scrambled eggs and rye toast at the diner.

"Is there any other way to meet men?" we all asked. No. Not really.

At meet-ups, we nursed drinks and shared plates of french fries and clams casino, all the while running our eyes over the men who came in, as they eyed us too. Once in a while, I'd joke that this was Dante's 10th circle, and we'd all laugh, and I wouldn't tell them that I meant it. Once in a while, Denise, ever optimistic, would say, "Smile, you're so much prettier when you smile," and I'd ignore the backhanded compliment, plaster on a Mary Tyler Moore all-tooth grin, even though it looked much better on Mary Tyler Moore than on me.

Once in a while, it did the job, would catch a man's eye. He'd nod, I'd nod. He'd join me and exchange the expected small talk: "My name is___, I work for (fill in any one of the corporations that dotted the landscape where I lived). Oh, you do too? What building? Yes, I have one, a daughter, six now. No, you don't have kids? You like drag racing?" And five minutes in, we'd realize at the same time that we had nothing in common, not one thing, and we'd both step back, drift away from each other while I contemplated the door.

I remember how Krys was when we went out together, tall and willowy, elegant and graceful, how she danced with first one eager man, then another, her smile inviting, her long blond hair swinging as this one or that one spun her around on the dance floor and she threw her head back, laughing. She was lovely. Instinctively, she knew the dating rituals that I was never good at. I wished I could be as easygoing as she was.

I love dancing. But not with strangers.

Sometimes, more than sometimes, when I was dancing or talking with a man I knew I'd never see again, I thought of my preteen daughter and the lost hours I'd rather have spent at home with her, sharing white pizza from Ridge Pizzeria, curled up on the couch watching PBS's *Ann of Green Gables* for the twentieth time. I'd ask myself, do I really have to do this? Maybe, it's better just to accept that I will be single for the rest of my life and get on with it.

And I'd stop going out for a while, six months, a year, sometimes more. Until I remembered that I liked the promise of marriage, the warm familiarity of loving that one man who fit me, the easiness of it, the day-to-day routine of knowing that, no matter how bad my day is, I will see him for dinner, throw a meal together from whatever is in the fridge. And, after, curl up next to him watching the news or a movie, reading a book or the newspaper, knowing we will tuck into bed together and I will breathe in the smell of him, taste his kiss, fall asleep touching him. And grow old with him. I missed that part of it. I longed for the Carrie Fischer moment in the movie *When Harry Met Sally* when she says to her fiancé "Tell me I'll never have to be out there again."

Did I really have to do this? Yes.

And there I was yet again, meeting Denise or Diane or Nancy, a glass of chardonnay please, huddled together at a table, jaded now, wearily kvetching about favorite topics, "the trouble with the exes is that they (fill in the blanks) don't see the kids enough, see the kids too much, miss child support payments, aren't there when you need them." Or "the trouble with men is that they" (fill in the blanks) want to date other women, want to commit, don't want to commit, want to settle down, won't settle down, don't make enough money, don't have a good job." Of course, we met no men on those nights.

Then, discouraged, I'd stop going out. I often did, with the job and corporate politics and deadlines, overtime and new assignments and crises, bills to pay, college to save for. There was my daughter, and school and summer camp, then after school sitters, homework and tutoring and orthodontist appointments, and allergy shots, and after school activities and lately applying to colleges. There were skinny teenage boys with slicked back hair, dressed in jeans and shirts with their shirt tails out who knocked on our door, parties and dates and movie nights out with her girlfriends, while I stayed home by the phone, fingers crossed, to be there just in case, no drinking, I hoped. There was carpooling and her own private drop off and pick up service (me) to and from school, to the mall, slumber parties, movies with friends, and, summers, trips up to Cape Cod to see Grandma and Grandpa. And there was being always behind, always a little late, always a little tired, too tired to think of time ticking by.

No one tells you how fast time ticks by.

My world was shrinking, my daughter was off in college, my mother had died, my father was seven hours away in New Hampshire and I was 46, fifteen years single. What was I doing? The house was so still, I longed for my cat to meow a greeting, knock over a vase, anything to make a noise, any noise.

And, when the loneliness set in like the hard cold in my bones on a January day, I'd give in and go out again, this time by myself to a Friday night dance in another fluorescent lit VFW barn of a hall on Rte 22, where it was déjà vu, conversations conducted in shouts over the thump of whatever tunes were in that day. Friday night, I and other bright cheeked women with gold hoop earrings and white silk blouses and hopeful faces clutched glasses of Chardonnay and hugged the wall in a single file line or gathered around the appetizer table and picked at the food, watching as men in sports jackets and khakis circled, took their time checking the merchandise. Because, if we were to be honest, that's what we were, all of us, men and women. Then, there I was with this presentable guy, slow dancing, smiling and nodding because I'd run out of things to say, and then he was pulling me too close and his hands were sweaty (were mine sweaty, too?). And I wondered, when the evening ended, what did he expect, what did I want? Was it me he was seeing or was I just a one-night stand? One pushy, sloppy kiss was the answer. Too much, too soon. I fled.

It's funny how life is, how things can stay the same, it seems like forever, and you can wish and want and hope and still nothing changes. But you persist.

So there I was, alone again, at one more dance, on one more Friday night at the Basking Ridge Country Club in a too bright banquet room with its parquet floors and windowed walls overlooking the golf course's first tee, a room meant for wedding receptions and 50th anniversary celebrations, not singles dances. The DJ dished out oldies, three couples slow danced, and a dozen or so fortyish singles, mostly women, drifted in, lingered next to the bar. I stood near the appetizer table, nibbled on a carrot for something to do, smiled my best singles dance smile for no one in particular.

One half hour more, I promised myself and I'm done, home, curled up on the couch with a good book or in front of the TV until the next time, not too soon, I hoped.

Not looking, still thinking about leaving, I stepped back, bumped into him. He laughed, then smiled at me, a bright lit-up smile. I laughed too, pretended I wasn't embarrassed. I liked the look of him, his broad shoulders and open face, short black curly hair falling across his forehead. I liked the kindness in his voice when he spoke of his young sons and asked about my daughter. I liked that he never once took his eyes off me while we were talking.

And, when we danced, this stranger and I, I liked the warmth of his hand in mine and the feel of his other hand in the small of my back, the feel of his body next to mine. Chemistry, connection, who can explain it? But it was there, that night.

It was only when he asked for a second dance and then a third and a fourth that I remembered what I had long forgotten, that the difference between before and after is only one second.

Call Back

Carole Schauer

When I arrive, six women are already there—five white, one black, ages forty to sixty-five years. They've already donned their green hospital gowns and wear them as instructed by the nurse, open to the front.

Anxiety in the group is running high. We all had received the dreaded letter asking us to call the hospital and arrange a second screening. Nervous chatter can be heard. "I've been called back before. One time they found a lump and had to do a biopsy, but it was benign."

Seven women together in one room waiting for their second mammogram is not a good place to be. We feed on each other's worry. Wouldn't it have made more sense to bring us back separately with women who are having their first screenings?

"I just dread this waiting. What did they find on the first one and why am I back?"

It feels like we're in a simmering cauldron. As each relates her story, the apprehension and disquiet heighten. On occasion nervous laughter bubbles up.

"I've been in remission for five years. What if they've found something?"

One by one we are called to leave the room. A short time later each returns and is told to wait to see if the screening was done correctly. If it was, you can dress and leave—still not knowing the outcome of the test.

Now it's my turn. I ask the technician why I've been called back. She tells me an enlarged node was found, and they want to recheck it. My anxiety jumps from five to seven, on a scale of one to ten. As mammograms go, this one was not too uncomfortable. At times I envision the experience to be like that of a car that is put into a crusher. Let's see how flat we can make you. At least the discomfort makes you forget about worrying.

Back in the waiting room, I see that our group is slowly dwindling as each leaves after completing her test. I wait. The black woman is told she needs an ultra sound. Then the technician tells me they have to do the mammogram again. My apprehension climbs to nine as I head to the screening room.

Back to the waiting room again, where I do just that—wait, on pins and needles. Suspense runs high among those of us who are left. Again, the technician comes back. She has consulted with the radiologist, who wants to do an ultra sound. She'll call me when they're ready. Boing! My anxiety is off the charts.

With a smile on her face, the black woman returns from her ultra sound and almost skips into the changing room to dress. From over the top of the curtain, I hear, "Thank you, Jesus!" As if a balloon has popped, the trepidation and unease in the room evaporates and smiles are seen.

Off I go for the ultrasound. Filled with dread, I wait thirty long minutes on the cold, uncomfortable table. As each minute ticks by, my panic climbs. Finally, the doctor arrives and does the test. Her final words are, "The node we see is a normal one in your armpit. You have nothing to worry about." Yes indeed, THANK YOU, JESUS.

Risk

Mimi S Dupont

Thank you, Friend, for choosing to be vulnerable with our writing group after your close (non-writer) friend criticized your essay. You asked an honest (writer) question: Is my writing too this or too that. I am grateful you asked. Here's why:

1. Your choice to be vulnerable reminded me to ask the right person.

Your request was sincere. Your question was honest. Your confidence was shaken the day you queried us. Your self-assurance had been assaulted from a direction you had not expected.

If you had sounded needy, been fishing for compliments, say, I might have felt resistance to your request and raised my emotional shield. If you had sounded angry, I might have felt angry, too. I might have reacted by defending you against your friend's hard words or by turning those words on you myself. If you had sounded defensive, I might have felt irritated and put off. Instead I felt invited into your dark place surrounded by the intimate trust of colleagues spread on the table like an open hand of cards.

Years ago, when I first began dealing—naively—with my then-husband's then-alcoholism, I went to him several times to discuss what I had been learning. He reacted each time with neediness, defensiveness or anger, all of which a counselor later told me were ways for him to avoid dealing with his problem. The counselor also said my needs were legitimate, but it was my responsibility to ask someone who could meet those needs in an emotionally healthy way. He was not that person at that time for that need. We both grew a lot over time.

So I learned this: When I need something, ask a person who is equipped to meet that need. My reminder came at your expense.

2. Your choice to be vulnerable reminded me of the difference between reacting and responding.

Reaction [ree-ak-shuh n] Noun. A reverse movement or tendency; an action in a reverse direction or manner; a response to stimulus.

Response [ri-spons] Noun. An answer or reply, as in words or some action.

The difference becomes evident when one considers what "responsible" means: having a capacity for moral decisions and therefore accountable; capable of rational thought or action. It's thinking that makes the difference. Being thought-full.

That realization has fueled my effort of 30-some years not to react, not to do what I'd always done, but to respond, to think and therefore to choose my reply or action, sometimes discarding several possible reactions as immature or inappropriate and going with, perhaps, option number four, all before I open my mouth. It's an ongoing effort.

So I learned this: Ponder my response. Be intentional. Don't let my gut alone dictate what I say or do. My reminder came because you reached out.

3. Your choice to be vulnerable reminded me to take the risk.

You risked rejection by asking a friend her opinion about your writing. You risked even more by asking us to evaluate your writing knowing your friend had already criticized your words. It occurs to me that criticizing and critiquing are inherently different. Criticizing is about the criticize-r. Critiquing is about the writing, not the individuals involved.

I am reminded of a moment in my mid-forties when, sitting in a circle among individuals of differing opinions, their voices receded and I heard only my inner voice of wisdom. Wisdom was calling me to be "publicly vulnerable." Those were the words I heard: "Are you willing to be publicly vulnerable?" In that moment. In my life. "Yes."

What is life without risk? Is there "life" in complete safety? A closed mind, an imprisoned heart, unnoticed because of blinders printed with "play it safe."

So I learned this: The result of taking risks isn't always going to be what we'd hoped. But for those who wish to live fully every moment before we draw our last breath, risk is playing our best hand and accepting the consequences whether it's a lost card game, a lost friendship, or a lost love.

Your risk inspired me, Friend. And I am so grateful.

Spinning at the Midway Gym

We pump our pedals going nowhere
at all with such lightness and grace,
as we turn mythical corners, climb
hills, race the obstacle course,
such aching, sweat-laced machines
churning away to Queen
who wants somebody to love.
In the mammoth mirror we face,
I see Shauna's baseball cap hide
hair loss from chemo,
Marilee's lavish ass spill
off the saddle, Joy's bony ribs push
against her tank top
while my jellied thighs hide
in snug spandex, lust
for hard muscle. All of us defy
the recurrent commands, the calls
to camouflage, suck, tuck,
gain, lose, limit sex to the dark,
cover the bumps, the lumps,
the pounds of flesh, shun the tight,
the bright, the light, bind
our psyches to the scale.
But not today. Today we spin.
Today we are gold. Today
we are beautiful.

Irene Fick

This poem was published in Irene Fick's new chapbook, *The Wild Side of the Window* (July 2018).

Side by Side

Carole Schauer

There they sat. A couple—close together, leaning slightly towards each other. Both appeared to be in their thirties; one with curly hair, one straight. One wore glasses, the other didn't.

The occasion was a church conference meeting. More than 500 clergy and laity were seated around tables all facing the dais. Our Bishop presided over worship, reports, and business. Speakers attempted to make their information lively and engaging for this rather staid and reserved crowd. Sometimes they succeeded; other times they did not. The proposed resolutions ranged from perfunctory to hot topics. It was for the latter that one saw a mad dash for the microphones—if one could say that winding and plodding one's way through the many tables was a mad dash—to offer positions for or against.

But, it was the couple that caught my eye. Now, fifteen years widowed, I find twosomes captivating to watch. Part of me does so with wistfulness—watching and coveting something I no longer have. Another piece of me conjures up images of what is being felt, said, or not said between them. At other times when I hear them complaining about each other, I berate them in my mind for not appreciating what they have because one day one of them will be alone.

The two sat there quietly, listening. Were they clergy, laity or both? It was the "leaning in" towards each other that spoke volumes. It made them a couple instead of two people just sitting side by side. Love, devotion, and acceptance were the words that came to mind as I watched them. Also, secrets and understandings. It was this I missed most—not having someone in my life who, after years of being together, knew by my glance or wink what I was thinking.

One reached out and laid a hand tenderly on the other's back—a gesture so common among couples, but usually taken for granted. This gentle signal seemed to say, "This is mine. We are together." The hand not only signaled possessiveness but offered commitment and comfort. It is a sign that marks two people a couple, and for those of us who aren't part of a couple, it sparks a yearning to be one. Even when seen from a distance, the hand touching the back of another announces that the two are connected by more than friendship; they are joined together in a special way.

She leaned closer and whispered in her ear. I watched and wondered what was said.

Advice from a Hummingbird

Yield to the allure of red. Be light-hearted.
Show off your aerobatics. Hover.
Fly backwards to see where you've been.

Learn from your mama. Defend your territory.
Build a tiny home—they're all the rage now.

Party with friends at nectar bars. Frolic
near verandas where wind chimes soothe. Embrace
your onomatopoetic name. Never be ashamed
to hum if you've forgotten the words.

Let your heart beat wildly. Find yourself
a flamboyant mate, a candy-colored dandy
willing to battle for your attention,
willing to woo you with endless serenades.

Fly light. Spend your winters in Panama
or the lush forests of Mexico. Exalt in tropical heat,
but always return to your roots.

From time to time surrender
to torpor, perching only if you must. Be yourself,
a jewel-hued nonconformist
who defies gravity, who finds reward in field work,
who dwells in her own radiance.

Gail Braune Comorat

She writes
because her mother is gone
      and their conversation still goes on

The Photograph on the Wall

Margaret Farrell Kirby

"I know why we try to keep the dead alive: we try to keep them alive in order to keep them with us. I also know that if we are to live ourselves, there comes a point at which we must relinquish the dead, let them go, keep them dead. Let them become the photograph on the table."
—Joan Didion, *The Year of Magical Thinking*

I sometimes see guests staring at a wall of framed photographs in our hallway. Along with the living—our children and grandchildren—are our parents, grandparents, aunts, and uncles, all who have died. My mother is in many pictures that span her life, from a young girl to old age. After she died, I would walk past the photos and see her gaze, forgetting for a moment she was dead. Each time I remembered, I was devastated, shocked again that she was gone. Although I had always expected that losing her would be traumatic, I'd never imagined how fixated on her death I would be and how big a part guilt would play in my grieving.

It was months before I was able to look at my mother's face without searing pain and longing, longer before I could relinquish her, relinquish my guilt and let her fade like the others on the wall, going with them to her place in time.

In April 1997, several years after my father died, my mother moved to Washington, D.C. from Florida, to a building for senior citizens close to stores, buses, and a subway stop; she said she felt like she was back in New York City where she grew up. After a period of fear and loneliness following the death of my father, she was happy; she loved living close to her family. She was eighty-two. She would have three months to live.

That summer, she flew to Boston to visit my sister and her family. In a photograph taken July 4, 1997, they are smiling and happy. It would be their last picture with her. On one of our phone calls during the visit, my mother talked about a friend who had died suddenly; she said it was how she wanted to die, dreading being in a nursing home or lingering with a lengthy illness. I said, "But Mom, I wouldn't get to say goodbye to you." We laughed when she said, "So long honey." She would have three more weeks to live. As she wished, she would die suddenly. I wouldn't get the chance to say good bye. She would be happy with how it ended. I would not.

Thursday, July 17, 1997. My mother and I took the subway—her first time on D.C.'s Metro—to the Department of Motor Vehicles for her to get a D.C. license. I dreaded the trip and the ordeal of waiting in line to get through the maze of requirements. On the escalator at the subway, she got annoyed when I said we needed to stand on the right so those in a hurry to get to work could go up on the left. She refused to move to the right. Then *I* got annoyed. My mother never lost her gritty Irish upbringing—she was funny, irreverent, and at times, stubborn.

We made it through the morning. After she got her license, I took her to lunch. She had her last hot fudge sundae. Then we went home to have a planned dinner with our children who gathered to see her after her trip to Boston. Worn out from the day, I dreaded it. We had seven children: a seven-year-old; three teenagers in the rebellious adolescent period, all at the same time; three in their early twenties who did not enjoy being with the teenagers. The dinners were often contentious affairs. I remember my mother saying, "There are so many personalities," as if to give a reason for the palpable tension. Exhausted, I longed for the day to be over as I half-listened to my mother tell a long story. One I'd heard before, more than once. I often wish I could return to that night and do it over.

I last saw her on Monday, July 21st for dinner with her at her apartment. Evening sun filled her balcony and her living room. The pink geraniums we had planted in May bloomed. The evening was light and pleasant, a lovely contrast to the earlier dinner—just the two of us and my seven-year-old daughter, Tierra. We played the game "Memory." We laughed. When we left, I hugged her and told her I loved her. There was no answer when I called her the next day, Tuesday. I figured she was out riding the bus or maybe the subway—refusing to move to the right. I hoped the harried commuters would be kind to her. That evening, when she still didn't answer the phone, I told myself she was with one of the friends she made, playing cards or attending an activity offered in her building.

When I still couldn't reach her by Wednesday afternoon, I called the front desk of her apartment and asked for someone to check on her. After they cut the chain on her door, they found her on the floor of her bathroom in her nightgown with the water in her sink running. When

I arrived, the paramedics were kind and gentle; they took me into her bathroom to show me she didn't suffer. Her body leaned against the toilet with her arms splayed out to her sides. If she'd struggled to get up, they told me, her arms would have been in a different position. They estimated she'd been dead for at least a day. Maybe two.

I can still picture the shocked expression on her face. I wondered if she had been afraid or had any inkling before she fell. As I sat on the bathroom floor and held her, I pushed her hair away from her eyes, cried, kissed her, and said, "I'm so sorry, Mom." At ten that night, after a priest had performed last rites and a doctor pronounced her dead, the mortician took her bagged body to the funeral home. I left and brought with me her purse with her wallet, her lipstick and Coty powder compact, her pouch with her rosary and tiny statues of Jesus, Joseph and Mary that I played with during Mass as a child. In bed at home, I curled into a fetal position and rocked back and forth until my husband came to bed and I forced myself to be still. That night, I remembered my first day of kindergarten when I cried and begged her not to leave me—she spent the morning outside the classroom where I could see her. She didn't leave me.

After making the funeral arrangements the next day, I went to her apartment in mid-afternoon. I remembered our excitement when we furnished it only three months before. The closed-up apartment already smelled musty. As I walked around, I looked at the chair I sat in, the one she sat in, at the dishes and wine glasses from our last dinner stacked neatly in the drain board. The sun glinted off the emptiness of the room. Out on the balcony the pink blossoms on the geraniums faded as the plant withered in the July heat.

I sat on her unmade bed and held her pillow to my face, trying to inhale her scent. Only the odor of laundry soap. I put it down and picked up a book from her nightstand—a self-help book opened to a chapter titled "Fear of Death." Had she read the chapter? *Why* was she reading it? Did she have a premonition? She would say things like, "It's getting close." Meaning that she was the last one still alive in her generation. We skirted the topic, or at least I did. I never asked her "Are you afraid?" Even after the light hearted *So Long Honey* conversation—a perfect opportunity—I didn't pursue it.

That day at her apartment, a deep guilt studded with remorse grabbed me and became a partner with my grief. Besides the pain of losing her, of having something vital amputated, was a conviction that I had abandoned her at the end.

It became crucial for me to mark the date and time of her death—was it July21st, 22nd or 23rd? I imagined it happened after I left Monday night while she got ready for bed, maybe while washing her face. Or perhaps Tuesday morning, and she was brushing her teeth. Or Tuesday night or Wednesday morning. I drove myself crazy.

"There was nothing you could have done," my sister and husband kept telling me. "That's how she wanted to die." Of course, I knew that. And I knew that if I had been with her at that moment when she fell and died, I wouldn't have done anything to cause her to linger or to be in pain. I would have held her, said goodbye, told her what a great mother she had been.

No one eased the tormented barrage of self-blame that assailed me. I could have gone sooner. I was the sibling who lived closest, only fifteen minutes from her. My brother and sister lived hours away. Anguished, I pictured her alone and dead on that cold hard bathroom floor with the water running. Because I'd been busy at work and at home, I convinced myself that she was fine; I didn't take the time to check on her when I couldn't reach her. It was a long and arduous process before I was able to laugh and blow bubbles at her grave with my siblings.

I had scheduled a four-week leave from work to spend August with my mother and Tierra before school would start. We planned all kinds of things: trips to museums, the monuments, a visit to my sister in Boston. My mother died the day before it was to begin. With no energy for the activities we planned, I wandered numbly around the house. I noticed the baseboards, walls, and rooms that were dingy, and I had an overpowering urge to cover the smudges and flaws that seemed to be everywhere. I bought brushes, rollers, and gallons of paint at a Duron store—white for the trim and tea biscuit for the walls. My husband said, "You can't just start painting: you need to tape the edges; the walls have to be cleaned and sanded; you need drop cloths." I just looked at him. During those four weeks I painted bathrooms, baseboards, the playroom, and the kitchen. Tierra helped; she and I painted a shed out back and made it her clubhouse. "Girls Only," she painted on the door.

My husband and children got worried about me. They didn't understand that I couldn't contain the energy of my grief. That I needed to create order in the chaos of my life. One morning as he left for work my husband said, "Promise me you won't paint today." I promised. As soon as he had gone, I pulled out the ladder and painted another bathroom.

Because anyone I talked to about my feelings tried to talk me out of my guilt, tried to make me feel better, I stopped talking about it. A therapist didn't help. The depth of my grief and my regret didn't translate into words. After I returned to work, I functioned on the surface, pushing myself through each day, putting on a facade of normality. But still, the heaviness I carried felt like a block of cement.

In the fall, about four months after my mother died, I bought a blank journal with a photograph of trees shrouded in a heavy fog on its cover. For weeks, I wrote and filled it with the words I couldn't say. I wrote a letter to my mother telling her what a blessing she'd been in my life. That first Christmas without her, I bought new ornaments—large shiny blue globes—and clear light bulbs. Something different, I thought, tired of our old multicolored jumble of ornaments. It wasn't until one of my children said, "A blue Christmas?" that I realized what I had done.

After the cold and barrenness of winter eased into spring, the heaviness began to lighten. The searing pain and longing her photographs evoked ebbed, and I could gaze at her. But I hated it. Hated when walking by her wasn't such a shock—it meant she was receding. Like another leaving. I wanted the immediacy, the intensity of the raw ache to keep her close. "Don't leave me," I begged, just like I had on my first day of kindergarten.

Eventually I realized that I needed to return to my life. I had to stop reliving the weeks and days up to her death and to stop obsessing over how she died. I had to let go of my guilt and my regrets: that she died alone on her bathroom floor and stayed there for God knows how long; that I would never know the day and time of her death; that I hadn't spent more time with her or listened more closely to her stories; that I hadn't said goodbye. I had to accept that it was her time to leave. She left the way she wanted. I had to let her go—let her become the photograph on the wall.

I gathered her things: the purse with her makeup, the clothes she wore on the last day, the book from her bed, the statues and her rosary, and put them in a drawer. I let her join the others on the wall and go to her place in time.

There is another photo on the wall. My brother, sister, and our families are at my mother's grave on a sunny day in the spring, eight months after she died. We're laughing and blowing bubbles. My children are a bit horrified–they think it's funny, but *really* weird. I know my mother would have loved it.

As I left that day, and each time I end my visit to the cemetery, I wave and say,
So long, honey!"

"Hope in the beginning feels like such a violation of the loss and yet without it we couldn't survive." –Gail Caldwell: *Let's Take the Long Way Home*

Another Mother

Mom viewed nature as a foreign shore, repulsed
by wormy soil browning her fingers, birds

spewing shit on canvas lawn chairs, the whims
of fresh air ruffling her rooted hair. Once,

she tried hard to beautify our backyard, plant
a row of zinnias in dirt laced with insects.

She looked so pretty in her outdoor ensemble:
powder blue pedal pushers, matching blouse, mules

that flaunted polished nails. A Virginia Slim hung
from painted lips, ashes snaking toward the earth.

I sighed, wished for a different mother:
a simple woman at ease in the dirt, who beckoned

me home to a scented kitchen, served honey-baked
ham on real plates. I think of this now as I curse

those damned portulacas I planted weeks ago
under a genial sun. Tending them with care, I waited

for the promised bloom, proof I was not
my mother's child. Instead, I drowned them

with the watering can, watched them wilt
under a taunting sun. I suppose I mourn those flowers,

just as I mourn for Mom, for the time she buried
her nature, tried hard to feel at home in the dirt.

Irene Fick

This poem was published in Irene Fick's new chapbook, *The Wild Side of the Window* (July 2018). It was first published in the University of Delaware *Random Acts of Poetry* collection.

Mother

Faith Lord

Color of Eyes?

I call her "Mother," on occasion, "Mom," but never "Mommy." Even the word Mother feels uncomfortable rolling around in my mouth. Four-feet, ten inches of solid Irish Catholic, she has porcelain white skin and hair a shade of slate—the color of the blackboard after one swipe of the eraser, to be exact. Although, it occurs to me that I can't tell you the color of my mother's eyes.

Fingerprints

Mother's reign begins in the womb. Apparently, she hogs most of the nutrients since she weighs twice as much as her twin sister, Dolly, at birth. Aunt Dolly has fiery red hair, but Mother is the fire and will burn to embers anyone who crosses her. Also, I know without asking that her fingerprints are all over her twin marrying my father's only brother.

Mother makes decisions for them both even now. She decides that she and Aunt Dolly are too fat. "You and I are going on a diet," she announces at the family dinner. In the end, Dolly loses fifteen pounds more than mother. She argues, "You've lost too much weight; you're sick." She immediately makes an appointment to take her sister to the doctor's. Out of mother's ear range, Aunt Dolly whispers, "And I cheated too."

Purple Mouth

Her twin, my father, or even the mayor of Baltimore is no match for my mother when she is on a mission. We kids contract a nasty stomach virus from the huge hole in our alley that collects the neighborhood garbage. Mother calls the city about filling the hole. She gets no response, so she paints all of our mouths with an extra layer of the bright purple, gag tasting Gentian Violet. One by one we step onto the number eight streetcar to downtown Baltimore and the office of the mayor. Passengers stare, then panic, pushing to a heap, and almost out the back of the car.

Six purple-mouth kids make for a clear path to the mayor's office. His startled secretary tries to stop us. Mother pushes past her and right up to his desk with us in tow. It is show-and-tell and Mother is doing the showing and the telling. She has us open our mouths and stick out our almost black tongues to display the popping red sores. The mayor's face changes from one animated gyration to another and he makes wailing noises similar to the Duffet's alley cat. He reaches in his pocket and pulls out money. Mother tells him, "I don't want your money. I want you to fix the holes in the Emerson Street alley." Eight o'clock Monday morning the cement truck arrives and fills the holes.

She Goes Too Far

Everything I do with my mother can be scary or embarrassing, even going to the movies. She has no tact and will push her way to the front of any line. I want to crawl into the cracks in the cement when she insists we change our age to match the lower admission price: "Faith, you're five." "But Mother, I'm seven," I argue. Getting it cheaper or free is better, she tells me.

Every charity in Baltimore has us on its list. She begs tickets to the theater, Christmas parties, and circus. We see magicians pull rabbits from top hats and women cut in two at the Hippodrome Theater. We also go with strange men called "Shriners" with tasseled caps, to see a clown being shot from a canon at the Barnum and Bailey Circus.

Not that this is all bad stuff. I love dolls, candy, magicians, and hot dogs, but even I know that we are not a fit for the children's Christmas party at the hospital. The kids wear PJ's, have liquid dripping in their arm, and lay in rolling beds. We have ribbons in our hair and have on our Sunday best—I'm just a kid, but sometimes I think she goes too far.

The Devil's Night

Halloween is Mother's favorite holiday. We wear her handmade majorette costumes. She and my father decided on last year's Tarzan and Jane suits that she made from an old fur coat found at the thrift store.

The nuns at our school say that Halloween is the night of the devil. Mother considers herself a devout Catholic and never misses mass on Sunday, but it would take more than a nun to intimidate my mother into that belief.

Like the time she made us all shorts and matching halter tops for St. Vincent DePaul camp. While filling out the paperwork, we chatter on to the nuns about the short sets. Sister Loretta turns to Mother and says, "Oh, Mrs. Nicholls, the girls are not allowed to wear shorts to camp." Mother asks, "Why not?" Sister replies, "The Blessed Mother would frown on girls in shorts." Without hesitation Mother snaps back, "As far as I know the Blessed Mother never went to camp."

Criminal Ingenuity

Finding creative solutions comes easy for my Mother. Though Aunt Ida says some of Mother's ingenuity could land her in jail. An example: Her present job ends, she collects unemployment, while accepting another position using her sister's social security card. They have the same maiden and last names, being twins and married to brothers. Aunt Dolly is a stay-at-home-mom, so she has no clue that her identity has been stolen. Mother justifies it by saying she is building up Dolly's future income.

The Fun Stuff?

Where does she get her energy? Well, she saves hers and uses ours. Picnics and parades top her list of what she calls, "fun activities." Not having a car means we walk miles to the zoo, Fort McHenry, or Patapsco Park. Mother loads Annie and me down with metal coolers filled with glass bowls of potato salad, sandwiches, and the porcelain-lined thermos, already heavy before filling, with the sweetened tea. I hate these picnics.

The blue and cream-colored metal walker with the wooden seat and removable metal tray, made for one, holds two of the smallest kids. We shove bags crammed with plates, diapers, and other kid essentials between the handle and the seat. Lifting the walker up and down the high city curbs causes the foot tray to fall off every time. Annie and I pick up and repack everything and reassure our crying siblings. At the park, we clean the fire pit, find branches, and take the little ones to potty behind a bush. *Finally....* the sun is setting, mother still fresh as when we arrived, but Annie and I now drag tired cranky kids and dirty coolers back home.

It is one of the times that Mother complains that I seem to want to escape to anywhere but home—she is not mistaken.

Fan-Shaped Hankie

If I doubt the reason for my existence, I'm reminded on laundry day. Mother flat out hates housework. Today she dresses in her crisp white uniform decorated with the starched fan-shaped hankie on her lapel. She pins Grandmother's broach in the center to hold it in place and leaves the house to wait tables at the diner on Pratt Street.

Meanwhile, we are left to watch the kids, clean and do laundry. My sister and I get the others to line up kitchen chairs in the back yard. We unleash hose water to taped-together chair-rungs crusted with the past week's food and wipe sticky hand prints from tables devoid of any finish.

Upstairs we break the steady line to the one bathroom long enough to scrub away body fluids from areas used for more than their intended purpose.

Just six and seven, Annie and I attach the ringer washer-hose to the sink facet and turn on the water. With a pitcher, we fill the three galvanized tubs. We add bluing to one, bleach to another, and one has plain water.

It only takes once for Annie's hand to be sucked through the heavy rubber rollers for us all to learn not to hold on to a piece of clothing too long or to let go of the broken cast-iron wringer, which spins out of control at the level of our heads.

We finish and struggle to carry the heavy tubs into the backyard. The dirty water sloshes side-to-side, tips the tub, and floods the kitchen floor. In the yard, we turn the tubs upside down and balance ourselves on top. We try to hang the heavy bed clothes high enough off the dirty concrete. I can't wait to grow up, so I can leave in my white uniform with the fan-shaped hankie.

Favorite Moments

But somehow, she makes Christmas mornings on Emerson Street magical. Annie and I help sell trees on the corner of our street. As payment, Mr. Overton gives us one of the leftover seven-footers on Christmas Eve. We manage to drag it home. Mother helps us set it up in the corner of the living room. We work to hide all of its bare areas.

I never expect gifts wrapped in brightly colored paper with red bows. Instead, each of us has a chair or part of the sofa that becomes ours alone on Christmas morning. One constant is a new dress from Epstein's on Pratt Street—one of three times a year we get something new. The other two are Easter and the first day of school.

She sends us to bed, strings lights, tinsel, and our paper chain garland on the tree. She lays out the presents for the six of us around the room until the fading paint and bare-napped sofa is transformed into a scene from the May Company store window.

In the morning, she does not let us descend the stairs until she turns on the record player and puts down the needle to start Silent Night, turns on the tree lights and those strung around the room. The music plays as we walk single file, youngest first, and me last. It is my favorite moment of the year. I round the corner. First the sweetness of the music massages my inner ears. I then open my eyes to the explosion of color. The room has been transfigured from the black and white of Kansas into the wonder of Oz. I pray Heaven is at least similar to the sight before me.

It may be wishful thinking, but I feel special this Christmas. My two sisters have brand new, boxy, hard leather skates with thick blades in their chairs. I know my skates come from the Good Will store. Although used, the stitching on the soft leather is fine. The shoe has stamped designs in the leather and the metal above the very thin sharp blades have curvy cutouts. I am sure that these once belonged to someone who was a professional. Mother must know I love to skate and that these would be perfect for me. It is my second favorite moment of this year. I love my genuine figure skates and I guess, if I think about it, for today, I love my Mom.

Daughter

Sherri Wright

Wash clothes on Monday; hang sheets on the line; iron them when they still smell like outdoors. After school put on everyday clothes; wear your school clothes for a week; school shoes have to last all year; be grateful for hand-me-down skirts from your cousin. Speak up when I take you to 4-H; you'll never learn to make a pot holder sitting on that chair. If you bake a cake, hide it from the boys; they'll devour it before you can pack school lunches. No, no Wonder Bread; Oreos or Hershey Bars either; we aren't made of money; besides that stuff is not good for you. Go to Grandma's for sauna every Saturday night; girl cousins, aunts, and Grandma go after the men and the boys who left a cloud of hot steam. You have to take a sauna if you want to be really clean. Go to church every Sunday or you'll feel guilty all week; don't show your Sunday school friend your father's Jim Beam under the kitchen sink; Methodists don't drink. Get up early; get out of bed and start scrubbing the floors; on your hands and knees; we don't ever use a mop; do you want to live in a house with dirt in the corners; or like the Johnsons; their house smells like a barn; or lazy like the Dabys who don't get their cows milked until well after nine? Get up; iron your dad's work shirts; don't be careless: iron the backs of the sleeves, the collar, and the placket in front; work hard in school; the teacher is always right; except when she talks about the Catholics who drink and party every Saturday night; stop mimicking that Putikka girl's Finnish brogue. Do you want to sound like a dumb Finn? Gargle with salt water to fix your sore throat; we don't run to the doctor for every sniffle; we'll call Dr. Parker if you're not better in a week. It's really nothing to cry about; your friend isn't much if she didn't invite you to her party; do you want to be a silly girl like her; don't worry about 7th grade choir; you can sing in church. Bake the beef roast until it falls off the bone; not one bit pink; don't ruin the flavor with too much pepper or salt; pass the roast to Grandma and Grandpa before your brothers eat every piece; don't mumble when they say their silent prayer; don't gulp your food; it will think it's in a dog's stomach. Punch the bread dough and let it rise two or three times; knead it hard or the bread will be tough; take the cinnamon rolls out of the oven when the kids come home from school. Where are you going in that skimpy skirt? I didn't teach you to sew sexy and neither did 4-H; we can afford enough fabric to cover your knees; don't they have a dress code in your school? And rinse that purple out of your hair. Do you want to look cheap? Why do you want to go out with that boy? Just go with your brother and the neighborhood kids; where is he from; what does his dad do; does he get good grades? And don't think for a minute you can run out when he honks the horn. I don't think he'll amount to much. Of course you'll go to the U; we pay our taxes don't we; we can't afford to put eight kids through college; you'll have to work your way through. Don't you want to make something of yourself? Your brothers will be engineers; you can be a nurse like I wanted to be or a teacher like your dad; until you get married and have kids. You know how to sew; make your own dress; prom dress, graduation dress, wedding dress too. If you ever have a daughter always sew her a new dress for the first day of school; do you expect her to learn anything in a tee shirt and ragged jeans? Yours were mostly red plaid with a round white collar.

Modeled after, "Girl" by Jamaica Kincaid

Beluga Pangaea

I.
Our guide sounds the gathering note.
   The boat leans as we all rush to see.

Outside, colors chatter, confuse
   in gray water, gray light. Are those
      whitecaps or belugas? Mothers or
         their gray blue calves?

Wind hisses across the foam
   a duet with sea canaries'
      coloratura whistles, clicks
         rising to the descant.

Whales slip around, over, under each
   other. Mothers' hydrocephalic heads crest
      while their small shadows curve,
         weave, unwilling to separate

II.

Each year belugas migrate thousands
   of miles south. Each year they return to
      this estuary where marine and riverine waters
         mix. Grown calves swim again with their mothers

until the old whales slip
   away as the old do,
      sinking quietly past the krill.

III.

I dreamed this dream when
    my mother was still living:

She is driving away from me, slowly.
She waves to me through the window,
a private, loving gesture known only to us.

Katherine Gekker

The Gift of Hope

Beth Ewell

In 2001, my husband Paul and I shared our first New Year's Eve. Instead of celebrating our new life together, I dragged Paul along to meet with social workers because I needed to move my mother into a nursing home.

I remember the wintry chill in the air, the gnawing ache in my stomach, the silence in the car during our forty-minute drive. Lost in my own thoughts, I stared through the glass window at fields where snow had laid a white blanket over sprawling farmland. It's a pretty drive, I'd thought to myself, but it's so far from my home. Did this facility even have a room available, I wonder. Would Mom adjust? Would she be safe? At that moment, a future filled with too much uncertainty frightened me. I prayed for guidance as I navigated the world of Alzheimer's disease.

The social worker, a petite soft-spoken woman, met us in the lobby for a tour of the facility. The elevator doors opened to Bing Crosby singing, "White Christmas," as we peeked into the formal dining room. Tables were dressed in red linens with matching napkins beside ivory dinner plates, crystal glassware sparkled against flickering candles. A hint of cinnamon lingered in the air. Lively chatter filled the room as men in suit jackets and women in holiday dresses ate roast beef and mashed potatoes covered with gravy.

"Mom can't live here in assisted living. She needs too much assistance," I whispered to Paul. My heart ached for what could've been had my parents moved to this facility together before my father's death. Perhaps things would've been less stressful for me compared to the musical chairs of the hired caregivers I'd arranged in their home—the ones that didn't show up, suddenly quit or took advantage of Mom's confusion and Dad's failing mobility.

Until Paul, I'd been a single parent working full-time, part of that "sandwich generation" raising two children and caring for elderly parents. In times of uncertainty when I felt completely hopeless, I leaned heavily on my faith. Could the church-run facility we were now visiting be the answer to my prayer?

"Can we visit the dementia unit?" I asked, my voice quivering.

We followed the social worker downstairs to a doorway where she pressed a buzzer. Tucked safely behind locked doors, nestled like a cocoon in a blanket of warmth, was the dementia unit. Residents sat on paisley pink and blue chairs watching *Animal Planet* on a large screen television within site of the nurses' station. I overheard an aide say, "Honey, it's lunchtime," as she assisted residents to the adjacent dining area for grilled cheese sandwiches and tomato soup.

Paul and I walked around the oval-shaped unit passing six private bedrooms on each side that surrounded a central activity area including a full kitchen with seating, an upright piano for worship services, and a large aquarium with neon blue tropical fish located near the only available bedroom.

I scanned that empty bedroom and imagined it decorated with Mom's things. A dark-stained mirror would be placed above her wooden dresser against the wall next to the bathroom. Her soft blue recliner would sit to the right of the twin-size hospital bed, and the van Gogh prints that she loved—*Harvest at La Crau* and *La Berceuse*—would hang on the wall next to the window draped with mauve pink curtains that faced an enclosed courtyard. A photograph in a gold frame would sit on her nightstand—the picture of Daddy wearing a gray, black and green striped tie that matched Mom's green suit—an expensive tie they'd laughed about that Mom insisted he buy to wear for their picture in the church directory. The last photograph that was taken of them together.

Everything *was* different now but as I looked around this room I tried to feel hopeful that the presence of Mom's things would bring her familiarity and comfort. Paul smiled, and I realized how grateful I was that I didn't have to do this alone.

A few weeks later I drove Mom to the nursing home. My stomach churned, and my hands shook as I pressed the buzzer outside the doorway. The charge nurse, Meg, a pleasant woman with glasses and hair pulled loosely into a bun, sat down on the armrest next to my mother who sat in her blue recliner. Meg wrapped her right arm around Mom's shoulder.

"I lost my mother when I was young. The residents *are* my family." Meg winked at me, then smiled and gently squeezed Mom's shoulder. Mom giggled. Did Meg notice when I brushed away a single tear that trickled down my cheek? I had just moved my mother for the second time in four years from another facility because of poor care. I hoped that things would be different this time, that after I moved Mom into this facility the words from the song, "Amazing Grace," *Tis grace hath brought me safe thus far*, would take on new meaning.

Somehow, I knew she'd be cared for by angels disguised as staff who would tuck her into a warm bed where she'd fall asleep to the soothing hum of the aquarium's filter, and I could finally rest knowing she was safe.

The following year I'd be diagnosed with cancer. Several months would pass before I could visit, but during that time, I never had to worry about my mother. If I called, the staff would put Mom on the telephone at the nurses' station, so I could say hello. On Valentine's Day, those angels sent *me* a card with a Polaroid snapshot of my mother placed in the center of a red heart made with construction paper that said, "Hi. Thinking about you, xxoo, Mom," which I proudly displayed between two magnets on my refrigerator.

I remember the time Mom broke her glasses and Meg had the frames replaced the same day. Another time the facility changed their policy and transitioned Mom to the skilled nursing unit because they thought she needed more care only to have the nurses' lobby for her return to the dementia unit a few months later. Was my hope being restored by the kindness of others?

Christmas 2003 would be my mother's last. On a blustery Tuesday in December I visited her on my day off from work. The dementia unit adorned with blue and gold decorations smelled like freshly baked chocolate chip cookies. The residents sang old-fashioned hymns and Christmas carols as they gathered around a table with the chaplain for their weekly worship service. I listened closely as my mother recited the entire Lord's Prayer and sang every word to "Away in a Manger," just like she had *before* when she still remembered me. Even residents who didn't sing or could barely speak tapped their feet or clapped their hands and played the piano. Music touched their hearts and awakened their souls. Could it be that the gift of hope was here all the time?

How could I have known I would find such peace inside that sweet little dementia unit, where the kindness of strangers will never be forgotten, and the promise of God's grace continues to bless me.

Old Woman Sleeps

On cool cotton sheets you shift
your worn-out limbs never sure
which partner will own you tonight.
These are potent dreams, dreams
where ghosts of old lovers linger,
many long dead or just missing.
Some once cradled you close
like rare and polished gold, spoke
unholy words. Others, bloodless
and tired, folded on your sheets.
So many lovers, lovers who faded,
lovers who wandered, no longer
craved your bed. You lost count
along the way. Now you sleep
the sleep of one weary from years
of coupling. Tonight, you slip
into the pure silk of solitude.

Irene Fick

This poem was published in Irene Fick's new chapbook, *The Wild Side of the Window* (July 2018). It was first published in the *Pittsburgh Poetry Review*.

Grandma's Pork Dinner

Faith Lord

My mother gets off the streetcar. She passes the slaughter house and heads towards our row home on Emerson Street. Half way down the block, she hears a grunting sound. She turns and thinks, "That's a strange looking dog." Its gait picks up and panic closes in; it's a boar! With horns and a knife in its throat, it moves fast in her direction.

She runs and jumps up on the marble steps. The door is locked—she doesn't have a key! She screams, "Mother, open the door." Grandmother hollers, "Go around the back." Now the boar is snorting at her heels. Mother's four-foot, ten-inch frame is beefy, but with the agility of a gymnast, she jumps the steps and somehow stays one pace ahead of the animal. She gets to the gate and it's tied.

Grandmother appears from out of the kitchen and quickly loosens the knot, she lets mother in but—she also wants that animal and its meat on our table. She pushes mother trying to get to the boar. Mother hip-pushes her back from the opening and locks a vice-grip on the gate. The boar rams the crimped metal over and over with his head threatening to break through. Just as an opening appears to be large enough for the wild thing to crash into our yard, a noose from out of nowhere is slipped on the boar's neck. And two men carry grandmother's pork dinner back to the slaughter house.

She writes to make sense of the world
because some days
    she is in a dark place
    and words are the only way out

Writing About Our Darkness

Mimi S Dupont

Laziness, or perhaps procrastination, is the armor I put on when I have to fight fear. I'll do anything to avoid writing about darkness, my own darkness. It's a lot like how I avoid cleaning bathrooms and baseboards. Do something else. Anything else. Clean out a closet, or a junk drawer. Take a screwdriver outside and replace the temporary tag on my new car with the permanent plate. Find all the gardening items in the garage and put them in one spot. Read. Do a puzzle. Do nothing. Do anything but what I know I must do.

Let fear surface, or not? As if I have any control over it. The most I can do is allow fear to rise and speak its piece. That's when I must say to myself: b-r-e-a-t-h-e.

When I do so, I can feel the tremble begin—small, very small—somewhere between the bottom of my trachea and the top of my lungs. Our respiratory systems are composed of airways and lungs. That's all. Two parts. But when we're trying to breathe, especially under duress, it's a lot more complicated than that. Some airways are as small as five millimeters. That's three sixteenths of an inch. You know: so many inches and three of those little lines, as a carpenter's helper once said when asked to measure for a cut.

I feel myself gasping for a breath deeper than … deeper than what? Deeper than the far end of my bronchia, not quite making the full journey into the oxygenated land of my lungs? Or successfully arriving in my lungs but restricted from continuing into my blood vessels? Shallow breathing allows no ease.

The fear of unleashing my fear begins as a tiny tremor in one of my body's weak spots, like an infinitesimal earthquake known only to me. I've never experienced an earthquake, except through others' tales; never heard the roar of a tornado, except on television; never seen the sky-splattering eruption of a volcano, except in video.

It's the power I'm afraid of. Power can be frightening. Fear strangling my airways like a boa constrictor. My anger overflowing into rage.

What would happen if I just sat down at the keyboard and started putting words on the page?

I've tried. Sometimes nothing comes. No words. Or words that carry no meaning. Weightless words. Useless words. Despair sets in. How do I plunge into my own toxic waste sites? Walk into my own lightless caves where rumbling comes from the dark recesses? Wade into the swamps of my own malaise, wondering what that malaise masks? Wanting to know. Not wanting to know.

In a free write, where writers gather for timed attempts to tackle a prompt, we were asked to write about a favorite children's book. This is what I wrote in four minutes:

Some pig!
Yup. Wilbur was wonderful
but Charlotte –
Charlotte was the most highly educated
widely read spider I have ever encountered
she was the cat's meow
the bee's knees
and like any good author
her writing came from within her
she strung out her opinions
for all her illiterate barn mates to see
left the farm family in wonder
at what her web proclaimed
at its wisdom
and what that meant for Wilbur …

Certainly Wilbur feared his fate. We all fear something, or many somethings. I finished my poem this way:

I never thought of this before
but maybe writing CAN save a life
maybe that life is my own

Angels in The Sand

Linda Federman

The heat from Susan's coffee leaks into the morning air as she watches a spider crawling on the outside of the porch screen. She stares so hard and so long at its black belly, that behind it the patio pavers blur. The landscaper wanted her to use the ugly concrete bricks he probably bought by the truckload for pennies. No. She wanted these. *Get them*, she said, *or I'll find someone else who will.*

And she was glad she had insisted; the awkward pie-shaped courtyard had turned out exactly the way she wanted it. Four sizes of rectangles in beigey pink, like the sand on a coral beach. A half-moon bar with strips of stone in gray, brown and that same sandy pink running vertically on its face stands parallel to a grill that rivals the size of a small car. Granite for which she'd scoured many stone yards top each of the bar's two levels; gray and brown veins shooting through a vanilla field, flecked with copper that winks in the sun.

Hydrangeas, fuzzy scotch broom and orange lilies spring from the border garden and spill over the edges; the silvery needles of a weeping blue atlas drape like a canopy over the oil-rubbed bronze bench. Colocasia, their giant leaves as big as faces, nod and bobble in orange pottery.

The sweet clarity of the morning is *too* ideal, nearly a cliché. Birds sing. Breezes caress. It is a perfect morning in the perfect courtyard, surrounding the perfect beach house for which she had ached her entire adult life.

She stares at the spider, the screen, the seams in the pavers disappearing, melting into a distant pink puddle. A puff of air conditioning slips across her ankles. *I should get up and shut the door to the house,* she thinks; *we are wasting energy.* But she is paralyzed.

She should be writing, working on her assignment for a class. She was going to write about Juliet. But she's buckling under the lead weight of profound depression. The pills are not helping. The therapy is not helping. The breathing and meditating and mindfulness exercises are not helping. Not drinking is definitely not helping; at least a glass of wine gave her a few hours of respite from the thoughts and anguish, sand-paper scraping in her brain. At least a Cosmopolitan unknotted the gripping ache in her windpipe and abdomen. But the doctors blamed liquor for contributing to the problem; they said alcohol itself is a depressant. Ironic, she thought, when the only time she could smile, laugh, exhale, forget herself was after a few drinks.

Depression sits on her chest like a bag of stones, pushing its weight into her lungs, daring her to breathe; filling her throat and guts, daring her to eat. Every day it gets harder and more exhausting to function, to be around people, to act like she's okay. She can't bear to provoke alarm; that only adds an overcoat of guilt; then she also becomes responsible for the worry and fretting of others. It was hard enough carrying around her own burden without adding the burden she would be to others if they knew.

Everything is perfect. Breathe.

Another sip of coffee and she asks the air how she will make it through this day. How she will make it through the next hour. There is a refrigerator full of food and good beer for her family, gathered here for the weekend. She feels the weight of that, too. Instead of bounty it feels like pressure. Instead of being grateful, she resents it. All the peeling, chopping, roasting, grilling, washing and drying dishes. Envisioning those labors unfurling before her is like pebbles raining down onto those rocks; she hears the tap, tap of them as they accumulate, feels them bearing down with enough pressure to turn her insides to coal.

Susan is supposed to be spending this quiet time finishing an essay, before her son and his girlfriend—who arrived last night—clomp down the stairs with messy hair, still groggy from sleep, hungry for mom's special French toast and legendary coffee. But how can she write anything at all when the stones have piled up high enough to create a wall? The wall is misery and it blocks out everything. It's blocking out the baby blue sky, the red twig dogwood, the birds alighting on the fence. She knows the blessings are there, but she sees them through a veil; she can't feel the joy of them. She knows the sun is radiant but can't feel it warm against her cheek.

Focus, she commands her brain. Even if you write something that sucks, at least you won't go to class empty-handed.

Write about Juliet.

Even then, just married and her own children still years in the future, Susan could tell.

The moment she drew her infant niece's little body to her chest she could feel it. All newborns are wiggly and limp, all seem unfocused at first. But Juliet was like a wet noodle, and the cloudiness in her eyes made it seem like she was looking way past this world and seeing angels.

What doctors had originally diagnosed as weak neck muscles turned out to be profound cerebral palsy. Spastic quadriplegia. Nearly half Juliet's brain was missing, and what remained was misshapen. Perhaps it was the result of some accident during gestation—an umbilical cord kink, a lack of oxygen, a broken gene—but no one would ever really know for sure. Her condition and its impact on her development begged all kinds of questions about God and fate. Why? All that suffering. *Why?* She was incredibly beautiful, and severely disabled. Wheelchair bound. Unable to feed herself or speak. Or even move much. Her limbs were rigid, her hands curled into tight claws.

No couple was better able to provide for Juliet than Susan's sister-in-law Hallie and her husband John. Medicine. Surgeries. Braces and joy-stick operated wheel chairs. All kinds of physical, speech and occupational therapy. Aides and caregivers. Love. Patience. Every day, day in and day out.

They didn't have a lot of space to ponder what went wrong, or why. Susan had the luxury of being philosophical, but Hallie and John had work to do. They also had sons to guide through childhood, two fair-haired boys with their own needs within a family facing extraordinary challenges.

Loved to distraction, a miracle child, an unexpected surprise; a girl after two boys, her arrival giving rise to a sense that the family was complete, even with her special needs. Or maybe she was loved even more because of them.

Then, when she was six years old, Juliet died of a brain tumor.

The family mourned her, honored her life and her memory with memorial ceremonies, with sapling trees planted in front of hospitals where she'd been treated, with benches bearing her name, with photos framed and displayed in the homes of each aunt, uncle, cousin. They remembered how her smile was warm enough to melt butter, her golden hair, her determination. They remembered all the surgeries and therapies she'd suffered. And then they all moved forward.

Twenty years later, Hallie and Susan are walking along the beach just after dawn, legs bare to catch the summer warmth. The sun has just begun its ascent, pushing pale blues and pinks past the horizon and down to the ocean at the same time, uniting sky and sea. The gulls circle, wailing and pecking for wayward popcorn and bread crusts. The beachcomber rumbles over the sand, leaving tractor marks like long ribbons in its wake.

How Hallie had endured, even thrived, is beyond Susan's understanding. As they shuffle through the caressing tide, fans of clear water kicking up behind their feet, they chatter about nothing as the pink sky gives way to brilliant blue, the ageless ocean spread before them like outstretched arms. Susan feels the sun and the salt lift her mood a little, like a crack in the wall through which a few beams of light pierce. She also feels somewhat obligated to be lighter in Hallie's presence even if she is pretending.

At this early hour, they have the entire beach almost to themselves; the crowds aren't marching in yet, haven't begun their descent to the shoreline, toy buckets and coolers clanging against beach chairs, flip flops bristling over gritty streets, clouds of coconut tanning lotion blending with the perfume of pine and brine.

A few yards ahead of them, a man of about thirty stands at the water's edge, holding a squirming baby in a pink polka-dot bathing suit with a ruffle around the waist, her upturned nose and round, peach-skin cheeks shadowed by a pink and white striped sun hat. The man's back is to the ocean, the calm gentle waves sneak up behind them and slide around his ankles with a sigh.

A brunette woman tries to get a shot of her husband and their baby daughter as the morning sky pulls the sun away from the graceful roll of the water. Hallie sees them struggle and offers to take a family photo for them.

"Oh, would you? That would be wonderful!" The mom hands Hallie her cell phone and takes her place in the pose, her hair dancing in the morning breeze.

"Baby, baby! Look up baby. Look over here baby. Look at the camera!" The tiny pink girl is more interested in the shush and bubble of the water at her parents' feet than the task at hand.

"What's the baby's name?" Hallie asks, thinking that calling to her might get her to look at the camera, if only for a second.

"It's Juliet." At first Susan thinks she misheard. She thinks Hallie missed it too, because she doesn't seem to register a reaction. But Susan's arms prick with goose bumps, as if the wind had suddenly turned from the east, scraping cold against her skin, and the hairs at the top of her spine tingled.

"Oh?" Hallie—always so smooth, so composed, doesn't skip a beat, doesn't even cast a glance of acknowledgment in Susan's direction. "What a pretty name. How do you spell it?"

"J-U-L-I-E-T."

The gooseflesh on Susan's arms tighten further into peaks, and the salt in her tears aches to join the salt in the ocean. On this whole beach, in this whole town, on all the nearly 100 days of summer, with thousands of visitors coming and going, how is it that the baby Hallie offered to take a picture of shared the name of her long-gone daughter?

"Juliet, Juliet. Look at me. Smile!" Hallie clicks off several shots, then hands the phone back to the young mother who glows with the innocent optimism of new parenthood. Smiles and thank-yous are exchanged. Hallie and Susan walk on as the delicate foam tickles their ankles. Susan feels small and humble in Hallie's shadow: how can a woman stand so tall in the face of so much tragedy and loss, while her own back is bowed almost every day from the weight of an amorphous, relentless depression? Most people in Hallie's situation would have been crushed by its enormity, its mass and heft, but Hallie powers on. It must have something to do with DNA; but could that kind of elastic resilience be learned if one is not born with it? Could Susan ever find a way to stretch that far and still rebound?

Susan can breathe deeply for a minute, feel the warm morning a little bit closer than usual. She thinks about how she has everything, and every reason to be grateful, not the least of which is her own healthy children. But just beneath the surface she continues to be plagued by a dark, enveloping sadness that blinds her, that obscures joy, that chases everyday angels and miracles into the shadows like a cloud drifting in front of the sun.

hurting heart

some days, your heart hurts
but a heart ache is hard to explain.
it's not a sprained ankle or sore shoulder.
there's no doctor's note or visible symptoms,
but you're limping all the same.

i am an advocate for heartaches.
some days, heartaches hurt more than
anything else you have ever felt.
some days, heartaches keep you in bed.
some days, heartaches are like headaches and
sometimes heartaches break you in half.
some days you are immobilized by something no one can see.
i am an advocate for understanding that to be okay.

today, my heart hurts.
i don't know how to explain how a mental and emotional
part of my being displays itself within me physically.
i don't know why not being able to explain something
makes it invalid.
my thoughts in my brain are making my heart hurt in my chest.
it's all connected and i don't have an answer.

but i know that my mind
my memories
my mistakes
and the mistakes in the way people have treated me,

make my heart hurt.

it didn't hurt yesterday.
hopefully it won't tomorrow.
but today it does,
and just because i can't explain it doesn't mean i don't feel it.

so if you wake up and your heart hurts,
if you slip and twist your heart the way you would your ankle,
if you feel a soreness from the inside out,
don't ever feel like you have to explain yourself.

some days, your heart hurts.

today, mine does.
and i don't need anything from anyone
except for the understanding that
feelings are not meant to be hidden.
i haven't used a band-aid in years.

are you okay to admit when you don't feel okay?

happy human-ing.

some days, your heart hurts.
all i will say that I have gratefully learned:
remember the days that it doesn't hurt,
remember the joy exploding within you,
remember that
as clearly as you remember the days when it hurts.

Annie Plowman

The Pond

Rosa María Fernández

The heat in my car is blasting full on high, but nothing can take away the cold. I know what I want to do, what I have to do, what I will do; but I can't move. Then my self-hatred conquers the fear.

The Plan is perfect.

I walk to the bench. It is surrounded by tall bare trees, all bending at different angles, looking as if they want to be anywhere but here. Trying to rip themselves from the roots that bind them. Stretching in despair toward an uncaring cobalt sky.

Here it is. The pond. It is not a mill pond like so many others in this area. No. It's been here since the ice age, making it purer, more sanctioned to return me to my beginnings.

The wind blows tiny waves that catch the sun and sparkle like silver glitter on the choppy surface of the water. The air is cold, burns inside my chest, and chills my chapped cheeks and hands. It smells of earth and leaves and wood and something deep, wet and mysterious. Snow geese gather in a neighboring field, like a quilt of snow trying to cushion the earth from the hard blows of last night's icy pelting.

This is it. How did I get here? Life is a trickster. I am the simpleton who didn't see her betrayal coming. Now I'm relentless in my tortuous taunting. I am the innocent unfairly accused. The cliché. The social pariah who has committed no crime. Framed. Betrayed. The judge's unjust gavel smashed down on my near perfect life.

I remember the day so vividly. Going home defeated despite having been assured the judge had given me a light sentence because he believed me, not the betrayer. But still it ended. I walked into my home office, empty now of voices. I took down my diploma and professional license. That was the last thing to do in that room. I never entered it again except on the day I left the house that I thought had become my prison. I soon realized the prison was lodged inside me, not inside the house, and I could not escape it as easily as I'd escaped the solid walls.

I flagellated myself with regrets and cruelty. Beat myself with the loose tongues and pointing fingers of others…"that's the one, that's the one who lost her career, her license, her home, her everything because she is an imbecile." I felt their fingers stabbing my back, I felt their stares, I felt their accusations.

Nothing seems real anymore. I live a life outside myself. It is too dark inside the abyss, but I can't stop the ink inside from seeping out any longer. I can't run from the verdict. Why do I care, now?

The plan.

The plan is perfect.

I take a few pictures and drop my phone next to the edge of the pond, opened to the camera. I make skid marks in the mud to the water. I must make it look as if I'd slipped, so no one will know of my great transgression.

What will it feel like to drown? What will it feel like to hold my breath until I can't hold it any longer? To take a deep swallow of the frigid water? Feel it liberate me from the rage and hatred; releasing the wild, caged animal I've become? What will it feel like for the candle to finally blow out and there be nothing but darkness and quiet? Sweet, beautiful, deep, quiet.

The sunlight glistening on the rippling blue-gray surface of the water beckons me: "Come closer, dear, come in. You can do it. Join us. There is nothing to fear."

I take a step forward and watch as my favorite white and rainbow-colored high-top sneaker sinks deep in the mud and becomes covered in water. I take the next step. Both feet are covered in brackish water now. As I prepare to take my next and final step into the pond, a vision of my mother's face appears so close our noses almost touch. I see in her eyes, my eyes. I see in her eyes, my pain. I see in her eyes, a sadness even deeper than mine. I see in her eyes a strength I have somehow lost.

A circle of smoky-grey surrounds her pupils, the sign of wisdom born only of many years. In her eyes I see my Abuela's eyes and her mother before her and even further beyond. I see a lineage of women some standing tall, some bent, but none defeated. None broken.

I remember that my mother's people come from Galicia, the northwest part of Spain, where in the ancient world the women were so ferocious in battle even the Roman soldiers were frightened and told tales of these women when they returned home from years of conquests. These warriors had descended from the Amazons of Greece and had escaped from three slave ships killing their captors and spreading in tribes throughout the ancient world. The women of Galicia were known to be the fiercest of them all.

These are the women of my bloodline. These are my foremothers and sisters. These are my survivors, my fierce ancestors. How can I be the one to break the chain of a thousand strong women calling me, beckoning me to straighten my bent back? Imploring me to pick up my sword and shield and fight?

I step out of the pond, pick up my phone, and walk away. A survivor, my ancestors' daughter, an Amazon.

fog

in the fog of age and illness
      life has lost its clear sharp edge

it swirls about in normal places
      obscured by clouds, shifting mist

falling in and out of focus
      then is gone without a trace

lost amidst the dark, the dampness
      as if it never did exist

sounds are muffled then boom loudly
      steps behind keep closing in

where and what is my destination
      can i return, find life again?

voices heard but not acknowledged
      who and why are they here?

do they know i can not function
      beyond this space where i now live?

still they speak into opaqueness
      calling me not using words

steps keep coming getting closer
      not to harm, to hold, to mend

slowly edges begin to matter
      light displaces damp and fog

loved by many, arms enfold me
      bring me back, where i belong

jahill

Authenticity

Who am I?
Am I who I am?
Well, now I am.

Authenticity
took time though.
Seven decades
of years and months
weeks and days
hours and minutes and seconds:
Time.

I started by discarding
Who I wasn't,
Yet—for others—tried to be.
A repetitive process
requiring a lifetime
of continual
emotional excising,
heart-rending
reparation:
Pain.

Confusion visited as
Doubt brushed by,
Yet, a memory erupted…

If only I had trusted
my five-year-old sense
of who I was…, for I've found
 —through my search—
I am identical, now,
to that beloved child.
Truth.

Ruth Wanberg-Alcorn

A Beautiful Nothing

I have become
nothing

by a product of my environment
and what has occurred, around me.

There is an essential soul that need only be
remembered, before

nothing outside can be
is not what,
the life
can be
made into what.

For one to accept N-O! NO. no. No. and NO
for an answer.

Kyle, "part of acceptance"

WE'LL SEE

What is, truth
Truth is:
GOD'S TERRITORY
I'll live with God.
The God in everyone,

you can

Go

to God

but, I, the power
am

ALONE

with God
with and in myself.

Irene Emily Wanberg

She writes to keep her brother alive
She writes because when she feels alone
writing consoles her

Doors

Judy Wood

South Lyndeboro, New Hampshire

She closes the door of the barn and skips happily out into the sunshine. An old maple sap bucket draped over her arm is empty, but dangles with a jaunty sense of promise. She's tied a kerchief around her neck and a straw hat covers her pretty dark curls and shades her face. She races up the path, pail swinging, legs pumping, occasionally turning and grabbing up her hat that flies off her head as she races along. The low bushes are thick with the luscious deep blue berries hanging in clumps tantalizingly ready to be picked. She runs up and down the aisles of pickers until she spots him. He, as usual, is telling stories and making everyone laugh and enjoy the day's work while his fingers fly among the bushes plucking the fruit. He glances up and sees her and waves. She takes her spot next to him. The sun shines brighter.

Durham, New Hampshire

She opens the door to the bathroom and stumbles in shaking. Moments before she'd been sitting in her seat watching as he and his opponent exchanged blows. The punches had flown. She'd felt sick to her stomach and had made her way to the stalls and wanted to stay there shut in and alone. He promised this would be the last time. A quick payday and an easy opponent and he could stay in college one more semester. He needs the money. She hates the sport. Later, when he had washed up and was himself again, he tells her that it looked much worse than it really was. He laughs and jokes and teases her until she almost forgets how it had scared her.

Boston, Massachusetts

The door is ajar and from inside the room you can hear the clack, clack, clack of her fingers on an old Remington typewriter with one loose key. He can't afford to pay a secretary, so she happily fills in. She couldn't afford college, but she did go to Katy Gibbs and completed the one-year course. She laughs and tells him all her typed letters are perfect and she deserves a raise pretty soon. He smiles back and assures her that any moment they'd be in the money. Every morning she clutches her bag to her side as she rides the subway downtown. She goes even when it means getting off every other stop to 'toss her cookies' as she's expecting their first child. At lunch time, they eat the sandwiches she carefully packed that morning and spend those few leisure moments talking about their dreams for the future.

Jackson Heights, New York

The door to their tiny apartment is always double locked. When she gets home from work, her first stop is the mailbox. She has the key ready although her hand shakes with anticipation as she turns it in the lock. Hurrying inside their sparsely furnished room, she kicks off her shoes, pats the cushion, lowers herself onto the worn sofa—the one they'd salvaged from a street corner a week after they moved in—rips open the envelope, carefully takes out the pages and gives herself up to his news. He describes the other men, tells her how he and the others miss being in the war and, of course, ends every letter with paragraph after paragraph of how much he loves her and longs to be with her. Through his words, he makes her feel the sights and sounds of the sanitarium and that helps her feel a little bit closer to him. She hugs the letter to her chest and wipes away her tears.

Bayside, New York

He charges through the door to success. Everything he does, everything he touches brings him and therefore her closer to the dream. Each sales call he makes he treats with the same enthusiasm as the first one he'd ever gone on. Every person he meets he views as an opportunity to move his plan forward. He greets everything and everyone with an intensity that fills him up like helium in a balloon so that when full he soars higher and higher. She watches and marvels and glows with admiration and love. And it's working.

Sands Point, New York

She walks through the door of the airplane and follows him down the aisle to their seats. A dream trip and he had planned it all from the first-class cabin to the limo that met them at the tarmac. A European tour. She pulls her dreamy fur coat closer around her body and tucks herself into it like a bird settling into her nest. When they arrive at the hotel she holds his hand tightly as they walk through the lobby. He greets everyone with his easy confidence and winning warmth and she is so proud to be on his arm. Room service, down comforters, tea cookies, embroidered hand towels, lovely sweet-smelling soaps and lotions, complimentary books, and champagne with real crystal flutes. It's never ending, and she imagines this is how it feels to be a princess. They're a long way from the blueberry farm in South Lyndeboro. She marvels at his confidence in this unfamiliar world. He is her champion and she loves him so.

New York City

The metal holder on the door has the patient's name and a manila envelope with his medical history tucked inside. The smell is an assault of disinfectant sprayed liberally in the air, combined with starch and laundry detergent rising off frequently washed bedding. The recently removed food trays leave behind a stale scent of their own. The patient adds to the mixture; his breath letting go of the medicines he's swallowed many times a day. None of this matters to her. She hurries to his side and takes up her usual position. Chair pushed as close as possible, she takes his hand. His voice is so low that her face is almost part of his face as she bends forward to catch every precious word.

Washington, D.C.

The plaque on the door has her name in gold letters. She stares but doesn't see. They walk into the room. The younger woman holds her breath and holds her mother's arm as they move slowly forward. The kitchen, straight ahead, has the same cheery yellow tile. The same random herbs that were in the design on the wall before are there again. The same carpeting, the same furniture, the same pictures on the walls, the same TV sitting on its cart, the same knickknacks on the shelves; all the same. They smile at each other. The daughter suggests they sit and rest awhile. They do. The sky outside the sliding patio doors is grey and filled with the look of rain. The daughter wishes the sun would peek out. A few moments pass before the mother pushes herself up and stands in front of the couch. She says, "It's nice here. Thanks for bringing me. I want to go now. I think the people who live here won't want us here when they get back."

The mother's words hit and hurt. The daughter's disappointment is palpable. They had walked in on the same carpet, stared at the same pictures of the grandchildren, the same silver tea set polished like a mirror just as before. Same, same, same. Everything the same. But, nothing is really the same. Everything truly important is forever different. The mother's lover, her partner, her protector, her friend, her husband is gone. And along with him has flown her being. The pieces of her mind are tossed and jumbled, leaving her a shell with nothing to anchor it. The daughter looks at her and sees a small, frail, old woman; her clothes slightly wrinkled. She sees a tiny tear at the seam on the shoulder of her mother's sweater with the sleeves hanging unevenly down her skinny arms. None of these things possible before. Her face is both pale and blotched with dark spots, but the worst part is her eyes. Her eyes absent of warmth, absent of color, absent of focus. They are absent of life except for flashes of anger and confusion which come more and more frequently now. The daughter rises and takes her mother's arm. They turn and walk slowly out the door. The plaque with the name in gold letters tilts.

Dedicated to my parents, Lillian and Win Nichols.

Talking with My Mother

In the twenty years since you died
I frequently heard your voice in my head
Take a sweater
That skirt is too tight
Are you happy?

Sometimes, that voice escapes—
"They're crazy," I say
as I toss aside a designer handbag at Filene's,
shocked at the ridiculous price tag.
The tone, the attitude,
both yours

Your Yiddish expressions
fly out of my mouth without warning
"Schmuck," I yell when the
blue Buick ignores me and my dog
trying to cross the road.

"Schmutz," I declare
surveying my kitchen in daylight
My frumpy image in the dressing room
at Chico's pronounces the blouse a "shmatta"

I look in the mirror and your face
looks back
I'm as old as you were when
I thought of you as
an old lady

I think of everything I forgot to tell you
Anything
I forgot to tell you anything
Especially anything I thought
you didn't want to hear

I could hear the concern in your voice
after the divorce
Was I eating? Was I seeing anyone? Was I happy?

What would have happened if I'd told the truth?
I'm lonely
I'm fifty years old and clueless about dating
Would I have gotten advice I didn't need or want?
Or might you have said,
Darling, I know how you feel.
I love you, you know.
I know, I would have said.

Sarah Barnett

The Long Goodbye

He now lives in a nursing home. I live in the home we built and he loved so. He feels alone and trapped in his new residence. I feel alone and trapped in mine, a married woman with no partner. We have 28 years together. Now we are alone together. "For better or worse." Better is over; this is the worst. Living in limbo, each day his illness taking him farther from me. I miss the man I married. I honor him by remaining steadfast even as the hole in my heart grows larger each passing day. The long goodbye.

Ginny Daly

Published in *The Washington Post*, Sunday, August 8, 2004
"My Life as Haiku" in 100 words

Point Pleasant

Faith Lord

The July air blows freely through the open car windows and stops just as fast as the brakes on the loaded sedan. Car doors fly open. Nine animated kids spill out, talking and squealing one over the other.

Being twelve and the eldest of the group, including my four sisters, six-year-old brother, Charlsie, and Aunt Dolly's four boys, I pop the trunk. I yell, "Everyone grab something before you run off." There's towels, blankets, bathing suits, several heavy metal coolers filled with potato salad, fried chicken, and of course, beer.

I can't help pinching myself—a rented a cabin at Point Pleasant, on a creek off the Chesapeake, for a whole week. I stop a moment to smell the salt in the air and the clean fragrance of trees. Mother promises this will be our yearly vacation from Emerson Street; I want to believe her.

The twenty bunks in our cabin will be filled tonight with not only us, but also aunts, uncles, and kids related and not related by blood. The cabins have rows of bunk beds, lumpy mattresses, one bare light-bulb hanging from the ceiling, finger-poked holes in the screens, and wooden canopies that drop to cover the windows during a storm; some might call it a dump, but we won't. We happily cover the beds with blankets, dust away the cobwebs and dead bugs. Annie and I sweep the layer of sand out the screen door. Its tight spring snaps the door loudly behind each kid that enters or leaves. We negotiate who will sleep where.

The cabin settled, we all scurry to find and pull on our wool bathing suits. A hornet's swarm of kids runs the length of the dock and hits the water in one big splash. Girls squeal as the boys pull at them from beneath the water, all except Charlsie—he will *never* venture in water past the untanned line on his ankles. None of us can coax him from his cemented fear of water. He does like sitting on the wooden pier to watch the boats.

The creek has hundreds of Sunfish that glisten and dart in the shallow of the grasses. I give Annie and Beth a towel and instruct them to, "Hold opposite ends, drop it in the water, scoop, and lift." We catch a dozen fish a dip. We clean and scale the bite size morsels for cooking.

My cousins find dry branches for the fire pit. Dad washes the picnic table with bleach several times and then again. He does the same thing with carving knife, the spoons, and the plates. Uncle Vernon, his brother, openly complains about my father's obsessive routine. As he bites the flesh on the inside of his cheek, Dad turns from his brother and guzzles his beer.

This is sober Dad, but he is temporary. I like this dad. I like watching him move through his structured rituals with the grace and deliberateness of a dancer. Mother joins her brother-in-law in the ridicule and hollers, "Charles, stop bleaching everything so we can eat." Dad stops and downs another beer.

As the sun falls behind the trees, the open-air bar comes alive with people and the long haired, bare-foot musicians. The loud sounds of electric guitars and beating drums echo through trees and cabins. Even though our parents bring their own beer, a bar with music is a must in picking our first vacation. Annie and I with faces and backs as red as cooked crabs, gyrate on the weathered wood dance floor to the beat of "Jambalaya on the Bayou" along with parents and cousins. Charlsie runs and plays hide-and-seek around the building with the younger boys. The glowing bare bulbs sprinkled throughout the grounds and the Christmas lights strung around the bar are the only light.

The night gets darker and the music louder and faster. The dance floor is full. Then a sharp bellow cuts through the air silencing both dancers and band. A sailor, who looks drunk even to my twelve-year-old eyes comes screaming toward us, "Help! Help! Help!" He has pulled a boy from the water. He lays in the blackness at the end where boats are tied. My father runs to the pier. The flashlight hits the face of the boy. It's Charlsie.

The leaves on the trees are so still. The steamy night makes even the young breathless. Volunteer firemen arrive. A crowd gathers around Charlsie and closes off even more of his air. Mother runs and tries to break through the wall of people. No one will let her near my brother. They put him in the ambulance. They take him away and then return— the road is blocked. Mother screams, "Get him to the hospital." My father insists they are giving him too much oxygen; no one listens. The words, "*He's dead! He's dead!*" cut through the crowd. The words, he's dead, rip into my ears like thunder. I don't cry because it can't be true. I saw him running with Johnny and Ted around the cabins just minutes ago. My mother's agonizing wails vibrate through the air and across the creek. Uncle Vernon catches her before she collapses to the ground.

I'm angry at my father. He seems instantly sober and crying and I wonder for whom? As a drunk he's an untamed pit-bull; he uses his handmade whip on our bare backs and his fist on my little brother. And why is no one asking questions?

How did the sailor know my brother was in the water? Why was he on the pier? There are no lights. Why was Charlsie out there without my father? He hates the dark as much as he hates the water. Did the sailor knock my brother overboard?

They rush my father and mother off to I don't know where? Strangers help me pack our clothes into a brown bag, and I gather my siblings. Aunt Marie and Uncle Fred, not real blood relatives, take the five of us home with them. We kids fill the back seat of the big black sedan. We sit lumped together as a solid mass; no one talks during the forty-five-minute drive.

We arrive at their row home. Smoke is pouring out of the window of their basement. Inside, Bruce, their eighteen-year-old son, lays passed out drunk on a burning sofa, unaware of the flames that surround him. They remove their son from the inferno, basically unharmed—a blessing in the midst of hell since they had planned to spend the night at our cabin. They carry the burning sofa outside and hose it down to a wet pile of blackened char as the five of us remain in our frozen state in the back of the car awaiting the next horror.

Aunt Marie and Uncle Fred's basement is not a dark musty hole in the ground with a dirt floor. This basement has finished walls, nice furniture, ceilings high enough for Uncle Fred's six-foot frame, and a door that opens to an area to park their car.

We enter through the basement. Aunt Marie and I carry the sleeping bodies that dangle like rag dolls upstairs to the bedroom, an ascending vision. I become more fear-filled with every step. I don't know what to expect. Irene and Beth still wet the bed. Without telling Aunt Marie why, I insist that I sleep on the floor with those I can't trust to stay dry, and I put Annie and Joanie in the awesome bed. Even now, I am nervous for them; will one of them catch a toe in the lacy bedspread or drool on crisp white sheets? Oh no, I don't dare take chances with bed wetters tonight.

I finally give into sleep like the girls, after taking them more than once to pee. I close my eyes hoping to awake from this nightmare. I want so much to stroke my brother's face and run my fingers through the cowlicks that live in bunches throughout his coarse hair. I pray that I will hear the rhythmic thump, thump, thump of Charlsie's top bunk as it hits the wall in his closet size bedroom. I listen for the familiar sounds of "giddy-up" and "whoa" as he gallops on his make-believe horse through the night. I listen but the house is silent.

dance

the world as i know it has unalterably changed
out of step, out of balance, filled with much pain

a woman i loved who brought laughter to life
has gone into the void of the dark of the night

angry, confused, too weary to pray
burdened by grief i weep through the day

i run to the place where the sea meets the sand
to find what i've lost, put it back in my hand

broken and bent my knees on the ground
i know what i seek here cannot be found

a small ship approaches, it has come very far
its sails are transfigured by the light of a star

the star is quite ancient, it once showed us the way
to the birth place of hope where a small baby lay

as the craft turned, sailed back out to sea
the wind filled the sails, my friend's soul broke free

and left in its wake the essence of her
in my heart, in my mind, in my prayers, in that star

as i breath all this in, i knew it was true
when you hold someone close, they become part of you

the songs of our life are sung in duet
for all who we love, we do not forget

we sing now of tears, of sadness, of pain
soon her voice will join ours, we'll sing of laughter again

and there will then come a day when our song fills the air
a hand will hold mine that i know is not there

the voice of the singer is not there by chance
as she sings in my ear, it is time now, it is time now
to dance

jahill

Letter to the Deities

Dear Buddha, Jesus, Hindu, Sufi, Jewish mystics, Angels and Deities of Spiritual Stature with whom I am less acquainted,

Really? Ignore that second arrow?
The one that causes ten times the original pain.
My own thinking about the agony.
I am the cause of my suffering?
How convenient to blame the wounded for their misery!
Those hungry ghosts eating my insides, let them go too.
Held accountable for my own aberrant cells, so be it.
Too fat, too old, too damn hormonal and
Amen and turn the other cheek.

Okay I can go with the muddy pond
that nourishes the magnificent lotus blossom
and perhaps light coming from darkness.

Jesus, what consolation!
Just breathe in and out Buddha.

Living presently,
Jane

Jane Bender

Published posthumously for Jane O'Rourke Bender, August 4, 1946-September 25, 2016.

The Water's Edge

Katherine Winfield

Standing at the water's edge it feels as if I'm on a precipice—a precarious place between future and past, teetering on the present. A swell of anxiety rises inside me. I stare at the pale winter sun that casts a stream of liquid silver across the velvety ocean, the timid waves that peak and crash in a repetitive cadence, and the black Scoter duck, bobbing along with the current. I want to implant the images forever. I know I'm doing what's right, so why does my decision feel wrong?

I inhale, breathing in the briny air tinged with sulfur. I like the smell. It reminds me of childhood summers spent here at Bethany Beach. That smell is gone now in the summer and I'm not sure why. But today the air is redolent with that wonderful aroma and the beach is mine.

I fling my arms out and throw my head back, letting the brisk air sting my cheeks. It feels like a scene from a movie. The camera high above, panning across the expanse of ocean then focusing in, circling me. I spin around, pretending it's the view from the camera, shell-dotted sand, cobalt-blue sky, cottage roofs peaking over the dunes. All that's missing is the background music—a symphony of strings reaching a crescendo. I laugh, feeling silly, and look around making sure no one saw me. But I'm alone. "Alone." I say the word out loud. Being alone is my new state.

There were times when I'd fantasize about being alone. No kids. No husband. I'd feel giddy just thinking about having my own space, no one needing anything, no one wanting anything from me. It wasn't as if I was going to pull an Ann Tyler-move and daringly disappear. It was just a little dream now and then.

Ironically, it wasn't me who left. If I had it to do over again I never would've allowed my children to go away to college. No one told me they'd never come back, that they'd live halfway across the country, both doctors living in Denver. And my husband, just when we were beginning to remember why we married in the first place and could possibly see a blissful path into our golden years, dies. A heart attack. And now here I am. Alone. Except for Ralph, a two-year-old Lab, who's waiting patiently for me to throw the ball again.

People don't like you being alone. They treat you as if you have some kind of affliction. Something they have to fix. After my husband died, friends kept suggesting I sign up on one of those online dating sites or invited me to dinner parties where there always happened to be an acquaintance of theirs who coincidentally was single as well. And no matter how much I insisted I didn't want to date, no one seemed to listen. How could I possibly be happy alone?

It was two years ago. The holidays were over, and we'd been planning a trip in the spring to Ireland. A golf trip, something my husband had always wanted to do. I hated golf. I never told my husband though. I'd learned to play years ago so we could do something together with other couples. He loved that I played, buying me a set of clubs for Christmas, getting me lessons for my birthday. I don't know why I didn't tell him I hated the game.

I found him in his recliner. January. Early evening. I thought he was watching the news. For months I was angry at him for leaving me. I know, it wasn't his fault, but still I couldn't help it.

And then I was inundated with offers—friends asking me to play golf. I declined. I didn't tell them that I hated golf; somehow that seemed a betrayal of my husband, so they got it in their heads that I was lonely, and that's when the dinner invitations started. I gave in even though it felt foreign—dating—something I never thought I'd do again. I thought maybe everyone was right; maybe this was what you did when you lost a spouse. But after countless evenings with a fake grin plastered so hard on my face it made my teeth hurt, I turned down the offers.

I immersed myself in projects: I organized every closet in the house, painted the living room pewter beige (the new color according to the paint store guy), took up yoga. I told myself I was fine, and I'd forgiven my husband for dying, but I found myself dreading walking in my front door. But it wasn't because I was lonely. I had no purpose. My whole life I'd had a purpose. I was a mother, a wife, and businesswoman. I was a fixer. I got things done. I was the one who knew where everything was. *Mom, where's my lacrosse stick? Honey, where did I leave my golf magazine?* I made sure my children ate well, got a good education. I helped my husband run his business. It started as a temporary stint while I was studying to be a paralegal with hopes of being an attorney one day, but the next thing I knew I was running his office and 25 years had passed. The business had been my husband's dream, not mine and after he was gone it seemed pointless. I sold it, for a comfortable amount that could last the rest of my life if I managed it well. And that's when it really hit me—I had nothing to do.

A year ago, I surprised everyone by putting our house in the D.C. suburbs on the market, the house my children had grown up in, and I went to live in the old beach cottage in Bethany that had belonged to my mother. My mother had loved the beach, but I'd spent little time there since I was a child.

Now I glance down at Ralph and think back to that first day in the tiny cottage. I was filled with excitement and fear. The last day of January, a bitter-cold day that made me wonder what I was doing as I listened to the fierce ocean winds rattle the windows, looking out at the other houses on the street that were boarded up for winter, feeling like the last person on earth. But a part of me knew I'd made the right decision. And then I met Ralph when I was volunteering at the local animal shelter and I began to start a new life.

Except it's all about to change. Next week Ralph and I are moving to Colorado to live near my children. My son and his wife are expecting their first child in the spring. When I was out there for Christmas, they took me house hunting, a rental place until I find something more permanent, saying how much I'd love it out there. We could go hiking and camping together. The scenery is beautiful in a loud sort of way, like a colorful marching band with cymbals clanging and drums that reverberate in your chest, stealing your breath. But the whole time we drove through neighborhoods filled with A-frames and cozy cabins and they were telling me how much fun I'd have, I wanted to say, *what about the ocean?* But I didn't say anything, just like I never told my husband I hated golf, I didn't want to disappoint them.

Now though, I realize how much I love it here. I realize I don't want to leave. But wouldn't it be selfish for me to stay?

I love my children, but I've grown to love it here, the quiet, small-town feel in the winter, and even the clamoring hubbub in the summer, meeting new people every week. My life no longer feels purposeless. Granted, there are days when I miss my kids, but mostly I enjoy my solitude. And it surprises me because even when I used to fantasize about disappearing from the family and retreating on my own, I never imagined actually doing it. My family means more to me than anything. So, what's my dilemma?

As the days are getting closer to my move a nagging feeling has been tugging at me. I've tried to pinpoint my reasons for not wanting to move, and mostly they're little things like the joy I get from my morning walks on the beach with Ralph, the friends I've made volunteering, the excitement of curling up in my favorite chair at night to eat dinner and read. But I think the main reason is that I no longer feel as if I'm waiting. For so long I did what others expected of me and buried somewhere deep was a voice saying, *your time will come,* and now I think it has.

The sharp air scrapes at my face, bringing me back to the view, the rising sun, the glistening water. I can hear the background music again and I throw my head back with a wild, belly laugh because I don't have the answers. Ralph drops the ball at my feet and whines. As I reach down to pick it up, I spot in my peripheral vision a man walking along the beach. It's as if he came out of nowhere. I throw the ball, then wait for him to pass, hoping he won't stop. I need this time to sort things out.

Ralph runs toward the man, tail wagging, eager to make a new friend, oblivious to my apprehension. If I don't make eye contact he'll keep on walking. And did he see me spinning like a child just minutes ago? He stops and bends down, ruffling Ralph's coarse fur. I look away then give a glance as he picks up the ball and chucks it far down the beach. Ralph takes off after it.

"Nice dog."

"Thanks." I find myself studying his eyes, forgetting that moments ago I wanted nothing but to be alone with my thoughts. He has kind eyes. Fine lines etched like driftwood fan out at the corners. Within minutes we fall into conversation like old friends meeting on the street while he continues throwing Ralph the ball. He's a widower, who recently moved to the area. I tell him I'm moving to Denver. Just saying the words makes my stomach clench.

He raises his brow and gives me a curious squint. "Why Denver?"

"My children."

He gives a nod of understanding.

"It would be crazy not to move. I'm about to be a grandmother." I say the words, wanting him to tell me I'm making the right decision. Why I want the validation of a perfect stranger makes no sense to me, but he doesn't speak.

I glance over and he's gazing at the water. After a few minutes of silence, he says, "There's something about the ocean, like looking into another world. I could stare at it all day."

I follow his gaze, feeling the pull of the tide. "I hate golf." My words slip out without me realizing it. He gives a chuckle but doesn't respond. And it's then that I realize, I'm happy. Alone, yes, but truly happy with my life and I don't want to move. Maybe someday, but today this is where I want to be.

She writes to give shape to things
she will never understand

Autism, Abridged

Cynthia Gratz Campbell

Baby

"How did you get such an easy baby?" My twin sister Carla marvels at how easy my baby is, although I suspect she is a little bit jealous. Rose naps, eats and sleeps on a schedule, rarely cries, entertains herself in her crib with board books. "You lucked out! Both of mine were exhausting and *my* daughter didn't nap at all!"

Bye-bye

Time to say 'bye-bye' after a play date with my friend Lori and her daughter, Tess. The girls at two-and-a-half play side-by-side, while we moms enjoy coffee and conversation, mostly about our little girls. I'm holding Rose in my arms at the front door as they leave. "Wave bye-bye, bye-bye." Tess waves; Rose doesn't. She watches with her contented, placid smile, as they head to their car. As months pass and I take her hand to help her wave, she flips her feet up and down instead, with that same sweet smile. Old Dr. Wineland, our pediatrician tells me, "She's fine, just independent. Stop reading all those women's magazines."

Bye-bye: Two

Preschool starts in September, three months before her third birthday. She plays at the sand table, sits in circle time, paints large pictures, mostly birds—"purple duck." Weeks pass. She begins avoiding free play, turns her small chair to face the book corner and reads out loud, *The Lorax by Dr. Seuss*. Another week goes by. Rose continues to withdraw from the other children and group activities. When the teacher tries to engage her, she becomes upset, screams and cries. "Something is wrong," the teacher tells me on the phone. Then, gently, "You'll need to find a new school for next year."

She seems calmer at home. By November, I notice what I mentally call 'the dumb look.' She looks at me as if she doesn't remember the magic words. "Please" and "thank you." By December, the sweet, contented look I love fades into a blank stare. It's as if someone kidnapped my daughter and left this new enigmatic child behind. An early talker, she loses all speech before her third birthday on December 24. Bye-bye.

Clamor

Sometimes she screams and throws hours-long tantrums, me straddling her thrashing body to keep her from hurting either one of us. Both of us are flat out exhausted, almost catatonic afterwards. Autism can be loud and then quiet. But her father and I wish for words, for her to speak again, any words.

Fast forward to one year from diagnosis. Rose is now four. Her dad drives her from our Virginia home to the private preschool in Washington, D.C., near the National Zoo, every weekday morning in rush hour, crossing the Potomac River twice. I pick her up for the afternoon therapy rounds all over the Washington Metro area. At least four times a week.

This year has been an endurance test, a grueling schedule. Months after her fourth birthday she screams, "I hate you." I am stunned and elated.

Cure

Let me get this out of the way. There is no cure, though some charlatans have convinced weary, desperate parents that there is. There are therapies—lots of therapies for parents to assess. There is the possibility of improvement, of progress.

Diagnosis

There is no definitive test, no known cause, not now, not twenty years ago. Research continues for biological markers. There are hypotheses about causes. Diagnosis is subjective. Specialists test and observe my beautiful little girl, interpret her behavior and pronounce:

"The neurological tests are not conclusive, it could be a rare syndrome that attacks the language centers of the brain, but we can't diagnose for sure and there's no treatment. It's idiopathic. That means we don't know."

"She's missing a lot."

"It's a multi-system disorder."

"Here are the names of specialists we recommend for speech therapy, occupational therapy, play therapy, auditory therapy, nutritional therapy. You need to work to engage her for seven sessions of play therapy at home every day; aim for 20 minutes a session."

Diagnosis: Genetics

Some specialists think it's genetic with a possible environmental trigger. "Don't feel bad," one doctor tells me. "It's probably genetic."

Diagnosis: Labels

Three exhausting months later, the nutritionist says, "Call it 'autism' if you want to get any services from the school system."

The term autism is relatively new, used first in 1940 by Dr. Leo Kanner. The definition continues to change with each new edition of the DSM, a big manual of diagnoses for mental disorders, published by the American Psychiatric Association. Over time, the definition has become both more complex and more inclusive. In 1980 one of six symptoms was "pervasive lack of responsiveness..." The 2013 update is "deficits in social-emotional reciprocity..."

Autism is complicated. Very, very, very complicated.

Joy

Autism hasn't been unrelenting all of the time, just a lot of the time. There have been moments, hours, even days of joy. We have some wonderful childhood memories, especially after the adoption of our second daughter, Elena. She is 17 months old when we bring her home from Russia. Rose has just turned six and is talking again, happy to meet her sister at the airport. "You brought my little sister home."

We have pictures. The two girls at seven and two, sitting on the rocking horse in the living room, smiling. Rose is behind Elena with her arms encircling her little sister. "Giddyup!" Rose chasing Elena on the beach. The two of them are dressed up as George and Martha holding their American flags. Elena is wearing Martha's mob cap and Rose is wearing George's black tricorne hat. The girls at eleven and six, sitting side by side, having their faces painted at Disney World. Rose rubbed her purple tiger off, but not before their father snapped their picture. Elena kept her orange tiger on all day.

Rose loves the zoo and we visit scores of them over the years. We are regulars at the National Zoo after preschool. Her favorite stops are the pandas, elephants, giraffes and tigers. She carries her small field guide and shows the animals their photographs. The zoo is predictable; Rose knows what to expect.

Joy: Sibling Rivalry

"What's that bickering?" I check the living room. They're fighting over a toy. Oh, JOY, sibling rivalry. It's what typical siblings do. Yes!

Life: 2010

Our family of four moves for a second time in June from Virginia to Delaware to get better school services for Rose. School and adult services vary widely from state to state.

September: The girls are settled: Elena in 8th grade and Rose in high school. Elena, who deserves her own story, is a desperately unhappy 12-year-old, while 17-year-old Rose is thriving.

October: "You'll need a biopsy." The radiologist has just completed my ultrasound, after the inconclusive mammogram and MRI. It's cancer, I know it. It runs in my family.

I have surgery just before Christmas. Diagnosis and treatment plan: Stage 1, Her 2+, new super drug, Herceptin plus chemo and radiation. Prognosis: excellent.

"Don't die, Mommy. Don't die." Rose repeats this phrase every day for the year my treatment takes. "I won't die, Rose, not for a long, long time." I am fifty-nine. She is eighteen.

Mortality

I think of my own mortality every day from the day in 1996 when her father and I receive Rose's diagnosis. The signs are there all along. The day, at 11 months old, when she breaks her femur and doesn't cry; her inattention to noises, to her own name, perhaps a hearing impairment. She doesn't point or wave "bye-bye."

Even now, the tape in my head repeats again and again. "She needs me! She will always need me. I am weary, but I cannot die. I need to live as long as possible."

Rose

She is who she is.

She is twenty-five, beautiful and generally pretty happy. From a distance she looks typical. Up close, she is obviously different, quirky, literal, ingenuous, naïve, sometimes silly, trusting, unwary, uncritical, forgiving.

She works at a restaurant and a bakery for a total of fifteen hours each week with staff support from her day program. She decorates cakes, makes tartar sauce and fruit parfaits. She tires easily and needs a lot of sleep; she takes a nap most days after work. A very early riser, never wanting to be late for work, Rose is often ready for work at 6 AM for a 9 AM start time. Snuggled under the comforter in her Pepto-Bismol pink bedroom, always with a book, she still loves to read, mostly fantasy. She knows *The Lorax* by heart, having memorized it in preschool. She plans activities for the weekend. Her dad or I take her to the festivals: Tulip, Chocolate, Sea Witch.

When she was a little girl she would say, "most of my friends live in books." Now she says, "I want real friends."

Rose: Forever

She tells us for years, "I can't live with you forever, you know." We know. We know. There are no intentional communities, similar to the life care communities for folks over 55, for Rose, not in Delaware. Rose, her dad and I look at apartments near our home. We find one, undertake the huge project of decorating and moving her in. After the first year, she seems happy; she likes having her own place. She still needs support and we are there every morning and often for dinner. Finding a live-in roommate/assistant is incredibly challenging. It's a work in progress.

I worry about the future. When we're gone. I want to be hopeful. I want my broken heart to heal.

Rose: Words

Rose has a large vocabulary and an amazing memory, diverse interests from animals and birds to presidents and geography. She speaks in short declarative sentences, like the ones I've used telling our story. Figures of speech, like "get on the ball" are foreign. She is literal, like Amelia Bedelia and living with her all these years, we have become literal, too. "A Country Club is a place where people from other countries go."

Words: Church/Peace

She knows she is different, and other people—including the children in church—are aware that she is different. But she loves church and insists that we go every Sunday. Her favorite part is the passing of the peace, shaking hands, repeating "Peace be with you." She tries to connect with those around her. Church is scripted; Rose knows what's expected. She also loves Holy Communion. We sit in front, so we don't have to wait too long. One Sunday, after drinking the wine: "Ah, now I feel better."

Words: Talking in church

On a recent Sunday, she is upset in church. In her loud stage whisper, "It would be so much better if I didn't have *the disability.*" She does not like the word "autism," always uses the term "the disability." Pause. "I hate the disability. This disability is a curse, it's a curse." It is just the two of us and I am also feeling cursed, tears sliding over my cheeks, alone in the crowd. I want to leave. Rose wants to stay, so I am trapped, struggling to maintain control. I wish I could whisper, "Beam us up, Scotty," and be anywhere else.

Words

A lovely woman, sitting behind me, pats me on the shoulder at the end of the service. "You are a saint." I don't want to be a saint. I want to be a mother with a daughter other people can see as unique, as authentic, as beautiful inside and out, as a human being worth knowing.

If only they knew how hard Rose has worked to get to this place, to become *her,* to continue becoming *her.* If only they knew how incredibly hard I have worked to make her journey possible, how most of my waking hours are still consumed with planning, organizing, fighting for her life. I am not a saint, but a mother on this journey with her; and alongside her, to become *me.*

Outside the Lines

I am a carefully constructed combination of everything they have given me.

As I am writing this, the child I babysit for decides to decorate my page.

"Can I color your life?"
She asks me.

Yes, darling. Scribble away.

For being a thriving original, I often contemplate the formulas that created me, the chemistry that molded me, the intricate interactions that fed my being, and the five-year-olds who colored my page.

Scribble away.
Away with what SHOULD be done and away with the ingredients that feed no one.

It's time to eat at the table from which we deserve to be fed.

It is time for scribbles that blend together and equations that make imperfect sense.

It's my time.

I am her heartbrokenmidnightphone call.
I am his coffee in the morning.
I am my mother's ride to work.

I am my grandma's favorite person to buy slippers for.

And this child's favorite page to color.
I am the bane and light of my father's existence.

Put me in your laboratory and blow me up, boil me down, and find within me,
a million worlds, a million words.

A coloring book filled in by all the souls I've ever known.
And I have so many more pages to color.

Annie Plowman

Sadie's Legacy

Sarah Barnett

My mother needs a nap in the afternoon the way some people crave coffee in the morning or a martini at five. She sends me outside to play on our Bensonhurst street. On this fall day in 1948 our block, normally alive with roller skaters, stick-ball players and rope-jumpers, is abnormally quiet. The only person around is Sadie, an elderly neighbor who lives on the fourth floor of our walk-up apartment house. Dressed for shopping, Sadie stands holding her black leather purse in a gloved hand. Her blue-gray hair is permed into tight curls, a look that is echoed by her black Persian lamb jacket. Crimson lipstick, heavily applied to her turned down mouth, draws attention to her wrinkled face.

Across the street a young woman walks toward the "El," which hovers over 86th Street, our main shopping area. She is a Black woman. Negroes, for that is the politically correct term in this era when Jackie Robinson just began playing for the *Brooklyn Dodgers*, are not often seen in this part of Brooklyn where mostly everyone is Jewish or Italian. The woman is dressed in the fashion of the day—skirt and blouse, beige cloth coat, brown high-heeled shoes, stockings.

As the woman draws opposite her, Sadie raises a hand and calls out: "You—clean?"

What could she mean?

"Are you clean?" would be a full sentence, but Sadie can't be asking *that*, can she? When no response is returned, Sadie repeats her question twice, perhaps with a "hey," as in "Hey, you! You clean?"

Now I get it. She wants to know if the woman is a cleaning lady. I've heard my mother and her Mah Jong friends talk about the difficulty of getting good help, but I think Sadie has crossed a line. *If Jackie Robinson could play second base better than anyone, why should Sadie think this woman is a cleaning lady just because she's a Negro?*

I register Sadie's annoyed expression as she strains to make herself heard. The woman shakes her head, mouths "no," and moves on.

I need to say something to Sadie. I want to tell her about Jackie. I want to tell her that her hair is the wrong shade of blue and her lipstick makes her look like the scary Queen in Snow White. But I'm seven years old and lack the bravery it would take to challenge anyone, much less an older person.

Some sixty years later I'm still struggling with how to react to the Sadies of this world. Too often I opt for silence. At seven I couldn't confront Sadie, couldn't tell her that she'd made a complete fool of herself. Today, I want to do or say something that would make a difference.

Often I've wished for a symbol of my anger, perhaps a red flag I could pull out, fling on the ground like a football referee and shout, "Unnecessary ugliness."

Curiously, Sadie's spirit seems to have stalked me into adulthood.

It's 1985. My daughter Michele is a bridesmaid at her best friend's wedding. Michele's fiancé, Kevin, is the only African-American on the guest list. During the cocktail hour, I overhear a conversation between Kevin and the bartender, who is white. "How come you get to eat dinner with everyone?" the bartender says, not in a sociable way. Both question and attitude mystify me until I hear Kevin's quiet response: "You seem to think I'm the chauffeur here. You're mistaken. My girlfriend is in the wedding party."

I hope the bartender knows that now he's required to shrink to the size of an olive, jump into the nearest cocktail and disappear.

In due course Michele and Kevin marry and buy a home. We meet Sadie in the guise of an agent in the sales office of a model home. Addressing me first, he asks how he can help us. I nod at the young couple and Kevin says, "We'd like to look at the models."

The salesman moves in front of the entrance to the model home and asks, "What price range of home are you looking for?"

"What's the price of this model?" Kevin says.

He names a figure.

"That's about right."

"Have you checked with your bank to see if you qualify for a mortgage?"

"We're just looking today."

"Well, you need to know if you can qualify and…" Now he's babbling about getting a bank approval letter, closing costs, and the complicated process of home-buying.

I fantasize about pulling a gun out of my purse and blasting our way inside. But Kevin appears unfazed. "Can we just look at the models?" The salesman moves out of the way and Sadie is momentarily banished.

For the most part, things go smoothly for our family despite the occasional reminder that the world is not color blind. But when Michele and Kevin take the next logical step—parenthood—my stake in the Sadie wars increases dramatically.

My grandson and granddaughter, 14 and 11, have encountered a few Sadies, but their circle of family and friends provides shelter from possible "Sadie-isms" aimed at them from the world at large. Friends and neighbors are mostly white, but with the popularity of international adoptions, their circle includes children from China, Guatemala, Colombia and Africa. Kids in their sphere seem remarkably unconcerned about race. As the teenage years approach, life gets more complicated, and I fear Sadie is lurking somewhere just around the corner. She may appear in the guise of a teacher, a neighbor, a shopkeeper, even a friend. I can't be everywhere.

If you look, you'll see Sadie in her unfashionable fur coat, lingering in schools, restaurants, shopping centers, even the halls of Congress. Not long ago, the *Washington Post* reported that a freshman congressman mistook then Rep. Albert Wynn for a waiter in the House of Representatives members' dining room.

I am constantly on the lookout. When my grandchildren were younger I held their hands, wanting people to know that they belonged with me. As teenagers they run ahead or meander behind. I'm considering matching t-shirts that say, "I'm with Grammy."

My daughter and son-in-law take a different tack. When the family is out with others, the parents delight in mixing up the kids. Asian parent cuddles Black child; White child rides on Black parent's shoulders. Bystanders respond with perplexed looks, struggling to match kids with adults, as if the group is a Sudoku puzzle, and each person must be in the correct square.

I applaud my daughter and her family for sending the message to Sadies everywhere: "Does it really matter who goes with whom?"

What will it take to banish Sadie? Can she become as quaintly obsolete as Aunt Jemima or Amos and Andy? I think back to the day when I stood on that Brooklyn street with ungrandmotherly Sadie, and I want to go back and tell her a thing or two.

Specimen A

I didn't glow
I wasn't anywhere close to a
gleaming, pregnant goddess
I felt more like a science experiment
Specimen A—Parasite growing daily
to be observed, poked, prodded
and worse, rubbed

it is said that when a woman
is pregnant, her heart, feet, and uterus
increase in size, to care for the growing child
the feet and uterus I believe, because I saw
and I know in my rational mind
that my heart grew along with the baby
but I really wish I felt like it did

I've been told you should
avoid clichés while writing
and I'm sorry but
I felt heartless

pregnant was the very last
thing I wanted to be
and I'm going to say
the thing you're not
supposed to say

I didn't want my baby

and to those who say
that I "just didn't know it
at the time" I say bullshit

but to all of those who said
it would change
in that first skin to skin moment

to those who said
my world would stop on a dime
that time would slow down, stop,
and speed up all at once
that it's like no other love
you were right

the forsythia hedge was dormant when we left for the hospital
its bare branches waiting on those first warm days
when we pulled into the drive, now a family of four
on a spring like day in February, you could just see the yellow flowers
   blooming

Kelsey Dugan

Funeral for a Pronoun

Rita B. Nelson

I never thought when I delivered my beautiful baby boy in 1968 that someday he would become a she. Never. Who could conceive of such a thing? My sweet boy Christopher is now a talented, grown woman named Kristen, and I have written about our journey together in my book, *Always Kristen*.

She transitioned from male to female in 2000. I soon discovered using the proper pronoun with Kristen was one of the hardest things for me to master. Overnight it was expected that I would refer to him as "her." Let go of the pronoun "he," embrace the pronoun "she." After calling my son "he" for more than thirty years, it was near impossible to call him "she." Still is some days.

As the months dragged into years, I kept telling myself Christopher is dead, at least in name. The reality of it was that the "she" he became is still flourishing and thriving. I have wept three decades of tears as I keep reminding myself of this obvious fact. Not dead. Changed. Yes, a big deal. Yes, a big adjustment. To this day my emotions are all over the place as to whether I have fully accepted this transition. Some days, yes. Some days, not so much. Some days, no. I want to be that supportive, accepting mother, but sometimes it just doesn't happen.

I wish we had had a funeral for Christopher—the name, not the child—because there is a deep loss here and I have a need to bury it somewhere. As I reflected on that time almost eighteen years ago when I was grappling with how or why a person could become another gender, I realized I never said goodbye to Christopher, to him, to my son.

Humans need a ceremonial rite to bring them closure in difficult situations and to move on. We celebrate births, weddings, deaths, mitzvahs, and baptisms with rites and parties, so why not gender transitioning? Because the concept that a person might have a biological gender and a different psychological gender (gender dysphoria) was so hard for me to wrap my head around, perhaps this formal saying "goodbye" might have helped my transition to acceptance. It might have helped me reset the internal pronoun from him to her just by talking about him at the wake. Wakes are those times when we talk about the deceased, dredge up old stories, cry a lot, laugh a lot, and revel in our memories, some to keep and some to let drift away into the thin spaces of forever.

"He was always such a generous man," said the recipient of a loan.

"Did you know he smoked marijuana in eighth grade?" asked his boarding school roommate.

"He was a fabulous painter, I loved his pictures," said his college art teacher.

In my mind's eye, I have often imagined how Christopher's funeral might look. Well, at least the funeral of the "he" pronoun. It would not be in a church of course; there would be no "Celebration of Life," as they call funerals today, but it could have been a private rite in our home. We had a large family room, where thirty-two candles could have graced the window sill of the bay window to represent his age at his death. Lights would have been dimmed to church-like reverence. Two urns of deep red roses, representing love and grief, would grace each side of the mantle. We would have Holy Communion to invite the presence of God. There would have been music on the Steinway upright piano, but not the funereal kind—those dreadful dirges. No, this music would be contemporary and reflect Christopher's likes.

There wouldn't be a body. Christopher is not gone. Funny, at funerals I've attended it is said, "Life is not ended; it is only changed." Not ended, changed. I have to hold onto that thought, as it will be my sanity anchor. Neither Christopher nor his pronoun, have ended, only changed.

The pastor at the service would extol his virtues—his Romanesque facial features, his bold and beautiful strokes of paint flung on a canvass, the laughter he evoked from others, his gentle presence as he danced at his prom, his love of all nature. All the good things, none of the bad. There would be no commendation of his soul into heaven as in a usual funeral service. There would be no committal of his body into the ground. The service would only be a remembrance of a young man once alive, but no more. A pronoun never to be used again.

I would even manage to give a eulogy although I might not get through it. What would I say? I know it wasn't just the loss of the name, Christopher, or the pronoun, "he," but something much deeper. I remember trying to convince her father that Kristen was the same personality as Christopher, and he said, "Rita, you don't understand. This is about me losing a son." And then it hit me. I have lost my relationship with a son, a boy. It isn't only about pronouns.

There is a big difference between the relationship a mother has with a daughter and a son; different expectations, different goals, different talks about life, sex, disappointment, courage, futures. I would hope I could eulogize about the struggle of relating to my son as a daughter, a she, in a positive way. But I can only leave that eulogy to my imagination. Having delivered many funeral sermons, I know this eulogy would be the hardest one I would ever deliver. On the upside, however, I could also talk about gaining a daughter. Talk about how we would do girlie things together, shop for clothes, giggle, eat ice cream, cry together over a lost boyfriend. It would be good to eulogize this in a positive light, for the word "eulogize" means to praise, to laud, to glorify. What a wonderful way to bury the "he" and move on to the "she."

In my imagination, Kristen would also be in attendance at the funeral. She could even give her own eulogy, a first in funeral history. I wonder what she would say about the loss of the pronoun "he," the loss of her male persona. Would she feel any loss at all, or would it be more a sense of freedom for becoming "her?" Freedom from having to live with the expectations of a son, a male. Freedom to burn her male wardrobe. Freedom to wear female clothes, makeup, and to finally express herself as she had always wanted to be accepted, as a daughter, a female, a she. Perhaps this funeral would have liberated us all. Or at least helped us let go of the pronoun "he." We'll never know; the funeral never happened. The pronoun never got buried. Even today everyone's tongue occasionally lets loose with a him, he, or his when referring to Kristen. We feel guilty. She forgives. We keep trying.

Even after all these years, there are still many nights I try to understand her gender dysphoria. And I still spend many days letting go of a son who is now my daughter. But when the sun sets, and the moon rises, I realize the essence, the personality, the character that was Christopher will always be there as Kristen.

A funeral is not going to solve anything or help me transition into accepting a she rather than a he. I'm not sure what will help. Maybe just the tincture of time will be the healing balm.

Some days though, I just want my beautiful baby boy back.

storm

scouting clouds obscured the sun
cold temperatures drop dramatically
the storm arrives out of no where

half way into my 10k ski it started
to snow, the wind began to rise
and rise, then suddenly to roar

from an ordinary cross-country ski
i enter a maelstrom of cold,
wind and swirling snow

snow comes from everywhere
pelting my face like slivers of ice,
falling from above, swirling in all directions

i become enveloped in a world
of whiteness, attacked by a dragon
wind slashing about with cold talons

my mind muddled by the loss of
place, all landmarks missing from
sensual awareness

how do you navigate when all
pointers are gone? memory, reason,
divine intervention, help?

slowly, with great deliberation, you use
all you can muster. danger and risk
are everywhere

get out of the weather, stay on the trail,
do not fall into deep snow, do not ski
into the river, keep moving it is so cold

inch by inch, you pray, you recall
the map of the trail, you reason
where you should be,

it is taking so long, too long, the storm
will not let go, can i make it back? the
cold is unrelenting

exhaustion creeps in with the cold. L pole L
ski R pole R ski L pole L ski R pole R ski
stop, listen, ski again L pole L ski R pole

mom! mom! i stop to listen mom! mom!
what was that? then out of the swirling
snow steps my youngest son

he saw the brewing storm, knew i was out there

it has been almost twenty years since i was
caught in the storm. i no longer venture out
to ski on the high plains of the rockies

my son's appearance out of the wildness
to find and bring me home, is etched
forever on my soul

storms are not regulated to that venue, they
appear with out warning through out
our lives. we may recognize their symptoms
but misjudge their velocity

it is my son who is now caught in a maelstrom
of swirling currents, the dragon wind of uncertain
direction, slashing talons, plummeting control

would that i could reach out, to walk into the
whiteout of his confusion, safely bring him home
i pray, but the trail is lost to me

L pole L ski R pole R ski L pole L ski R pole
R ski stop, listen, ski again L pole L ski R pole
R ski...................

jahill

What Happens at Sephora

The scent of musk pulls us in. My daughter and I wander random aisles. She tests glitzy blue shadows on the back of her hand. She wants a neutral lipstick. A man in a plum shirt suggests a candy pink gloss. She sighs and shrugs. For me, he offers a makeover.

I ask him to do something with my eyes. He fluffs white powder over my lids and beneath. Voila! He offers a mirror and I see another me. A woman ten years younger, rested and bright-eyed.

I become eager to master the art of artifice. The makeup artist strokes my cheeks with Begonia Pollen. It gives me a glow from within, nothing false, just shy allure. I blush; I'm hooked, addicted. I'm a gambler willing to let it all ride.

I tell him I yearn for lush lips that say kiss me. Lips unafraid of flaunting their sexuality. A pop of raspberry or wine. His hand hovers over a rainbow array, settles on one that resembles a child's red crayon. Summer Geranium. Statement lips, a signature shade for me to buy, he announces, as he proceeds around the boundaries of my mouth.

My daughter's mouth and eyes widen as he draws, as he reshapes my smile.

I lift the mirror and see Bozo's mother. Too much, I say. My daughter shoves a wad of tissues into my hand. I wipe until my mouth aches. She shakes her head and sighs. We head to the checkout line, purchase our beauty in mime silence.

In the next department store, nothing tempts me. I see only costume pieces: flouncy shirts and striped pants that would only exaggerate the look my face wears. At the jewelry counter, I'm startled by my reflection: a marked woman forced to wear the scarlet stain of her vanity.

My daughter races toward racks of designer jeans, toward the newest trends, and I fall back, dumbstruck. How quickly she's learning to distance herself.

Gail Braune Comorat

Previously published in Phases of the Moon, Finishing Line Press, 2015.

Half of Two Is My Only One

Twin large brown orbs planted in sea of corkscrew platinum curls
Blinks   giggles   scribbles infant poetry
Under the gaze of angora kitty
Propped on pillows of turquoise   white ruffled trim
Captivates   pulls love from places in me   depths I hadn't known
Call her euphoria   call her bliss   call her joy   call her my miracle child.

Vivid memory of reddened sidewalk   first hope lost
Glaring lights above, wheeled in, that word, *miscarriage*,
Goodbye, little Miss, miss miss. I will miss you
That bleak night   I lost you   rolling, crushing, aching,
Miss   miss   miss you
The morning spent behind the cotton curtain
Message from cold wand to monitor
I'm   still   here.
Hear me? Beat detected. It's *you*. How?
An unexpected matching other, is no more,
But still there's   you,   you, my inexplicable child, you, my survivor.

And to think
You might have been two. Twins. Twice your joy.
Could I have contained it?
I refuse to count you as half of two
You are one   the only one   my one and only

Little finger passing over words beyond your years   first word   *book*
Paintbrush swashing over packing paper pad on splattered easel
Colors. I want to roll in them   laugh with this creative creature
My birth day surprise, wise-beyond-her-years-child
Twice the heart, the mind, the laughter
Does her *vanishing twin* reside within?
Half-gift   twice blessed.

My 19 inch long,   5 pound 13 ounce   12.28.82
Six weeks early girl
Small hands stretching for piano chords
Freckled nose snuggling into kitty fur
Little girl fascinated by Egyptian queen, Japanese characters
Stories told with grand expression   and those eyes
Passion for words, passion for notes,
Black marks on lines in music books
Kept in lifted lid of black gloss

Grown woman's hands now   type a book   free a soul
My traveling companion, old soul, no disciplining required
Philosopher who teaches me.
Lips that send a song into applauding crowds
Deft hands that play a keyboard tune
Lucid lecture lighting up learning minds

Writer   advocate for women's rights, people's rights   She Writes
Traveler to Tokyo.   Book tour to Europe.
Professor at a university in New York.
Call her genius, call her author, call her Kristen.
My counselor, my daughter, my friend

I unpack the tiny T-shirt in my hotel   pack and unpack
Thirty-five years after her   fragile first day
Angled little silver snaps   pure white cotton
Size of my out-stretched hand.
A flag raised to surrender to pure love
To celebrate the miracle.
The first miniature T-shirt my precious preemie wore.

Laughing at myself. Me, nearly seven decades
I've come to take the pint-size T-shirt everywhere,
Italy, Indonesia, Mexico, Montreal
Reminding me of miracles pack unpack

One. My only one. My one of a kind.
Not half of two   but two times one.
She
  fits me
    to a
      "T"

Kathleen L. Martens

Dedicated to my daughter, Kristen—advocate, author, teacher, editor, and friend.

She writes with renewed faith
        because she wants to remember
                to honor
because she is a witness

Return Ticket

Christy Walker Briedis

Sage

Sage stared out the scratched Amtrak window at the flickering afternoon light as the train barreled south toward her family home in Washington, D.C. The steady motion and rapid click of the rails had a rhythm that reminded her of the drums and gongs of her Balinese home. But the bleak sights that blurred by seemed alien and colorless after her ten-year absence. The crumbling backside of tenements and wind-blown, rain-soaked trash pushed against chain-link fences. Dead-end streets littered with broken bottles, old tires, and abandoned vehicles, stood in sharp contrast to the green of Bali, where she had settled down for the last three years.

In her beloved Bali, sweet-smelling frangipani and brilliant hibiscus bloomed along every roadway. Her neighbors swept streets clean with palm frond brooms. Cocoa-skinned people wrapped in flowing batik sarongs hurried along those pristine roads carrying fruit laden baskets balanced on their heads or water buckets on bamboo shoulder yolks. Smells and colors were intensified and glorified by the clean air and tropical sun. Motorized vehicles swerved and bumped along the roadways making room for the pedestrians hurrying to work or home—in contrast to the traffic jams her taxi had fought from the JFK airport to Penn Station.

When she saw the Delaware River from her train window, Sage thought of the narrow waterways in the place she now considered home. In Bali, rivers were crowded with people piling cargo on small boats and bartering their goods. Here on this broad river, only a solitary grey cargo freighter loaded with house-sized containers pushed its way up river to be offloaded by some large machine. No humans were in sight.

After years of Peace Corps work, traveling the world and following her passion for new cultures and exotic places, she'd discovered Bali. Sage hadn't intended to end up living there, but now she was reminded of why she didn't want to leave.

Raising her eyebrows and shaking her head, Sage realized while visiting her family she'd have to go back to being called *Peggy* and bear up under her family's expectations. Despite her invitations, none of her family had visited. Too out of the way they'd said. She had wished they would have explored her world, but they'd rarely shared her interest in the uncharted choices she preferred.

Grandmother, why *did* you send for me, Sage thought. You never really approved of me. Surely, they could have buried you without me traveling half-way around the world. Sage clasped her hands above her head leaning left and right, releasing the tension in her shoulders. Could she explain to her cousins that her connection to the earth and community were now rooted in the Balinese culture? If her Grandmother hadn't died and left ticket money for her return to the funeral, she'd still be in her Ubud village studio, collecting batiks for export and dancing with the children.

She'd been allowed to join in the children's class, learning the basics of their stylized movements in traditional dance. Like the ballet lessons in her youth, students trained in defined, numbered positions: quivering fingers on arched hands, raised, pointed toes, bent legs with wide, expressive eyes. Balinese dancing had captured her body and spirit—the exaggerated, nonverbal communication and emotions expressed in the quick fluid movements of each dance. The classes were orderly and disciplined, all the students wore precisely wrapped batik skirts to allow full leg movement with a single frangipani blossom behind the right ear. When the afternoon heat diminished, dancing was the highlight of each day. The swaying movements of her body had brought Sage as much pleasure as the giggling company of the village girls.

"Union Station, next stop."

Sage pulled her duffle bag down from overhead and rearranged her massive twist of red hair, tamed by black enamel chop-sticks, a trick she'd mastered to keep the heat off her neck. The train lurched to a stop. As Sage disembarked, she recalled her last conversations with her Grandmother.

"You've changed your first name?"

"Grandmother, you may have been happy as a Margaret, but with all the possibilities for nicknames, Marge, Maggie, Meg, why Peggy? It never suited me; I'm Sage now."

"Peggy? Your father's choice; I gave you *my* name, Margaret. And you inherited *my* long legs, and green eyes. But, just look at your freckles. Clearly, you've been in the sun without a hat, however, your red hair looks wonderful—long and curly. I once wore mine like that."

Sage pressed her lips together and compared herself to the people in the station. She imagined Grandmother asking, "What *is* that you're *wearing*, exactly?"

Even for the '70's she *was* looking rather bohemian—wide batik pants, usually worn by men in Bali, but so comfortable, a faded tank top, well yes, a bit see-through without a bra, a large leather belt slung low, and lace-up sandals. She ran her hands up each arm, causing her collection of silver bracelets to clink musically, as they tumbled to her wrists. She smiled, imagining the Balinese artist's hammer pounding the silver as she squatted nearby anticipating his creation.

"Grandmother, how could we look so similar and be so different? You always traveled in some proper tweed suit, jeweled broach and earrings. Your closet had more shoes than I'd ever seen, heels and boots, matching hats and handbags—oh, Grandmother, you always wore the *perfect* get-up."

"Your grandfather and I had important places to go. Remember, he called me Lady Astor? A wife can be a great asset to her husband, *which* I notice you have not managed to find. And all that training I gave you to ensure you'd be a proper young lady…wasted."

"Oh, those lessons. I remember you marching me up and down your hall with a book balanced on my head saying, 'posture, stand up straight, swing your arms gracefully'. I never seemed to get it right, Grandmother. Even my sneeze was too loud and lingering for your taste. Do you remember when you grabbed my upper arm, leaned down and warned me, 'no man will ever marry you if you sneeze like that'?"

I can still see you shaking your head and pushing your lips together—tight, like I imagine you're doing right now. Oh, Grandmother, if your life was so perfect, why did it feel like you were always expecting more? Sage remembered her grandmother shaking her head in dismissal when as a curious child Peggy had asked prying questions.

As Sage dragged her possessions up the escalator, the old feeling of being alienated from the world descended upon her.

After the memorial service Sage slouched in a low leather chair watching her cousins cluster around the bar and buffet. Dressed in their tailored black suits with exaggerated shoulders, slim skirts and spike heels, they simultaneously balanced plates and cocktails, while marshalling small children in smocked dresses or oxford shirts with clip-on ties. Her cousins were curious about Sage's life, taking her aside to ask her questions.

"Did you finally get a place with electricity, Peggy? How *do* you manage without a washing machine? I'd hire help."

Sage twisted a few tendrils of her hair, picturing her dented, galvanized wash basin and her wet, colorful sarongs drying over low bushes. "I get by."

"Peg, I hear you have a little export gig going. Any time you need some advertising advice, let me know. We've gone international." Her eldest male cousin deftly handed her his card.

How could she explain her business was a community effort? Profits were used to improve the village schools; she'd only taken the money she needed to live. He'd never get that. "Thanks, I'll remember." She was saved as her little nieces and nephews gathered around her.

"What's it like in the jungle, Aunt Peggy? Do you have a pet monkey?"

Crouching to their level, she teased, "Our little monkeys like to live free, in the trees. But sometimes they visit."

Her eldest cousin cut into the exchange. "When are you and that cute guy, Tarzan, coming home and starting a family? I wouldn't let that hunk out of my sight."

Sage rolled her eyes and took a large gulp of the wine that she had quickly snatched from the server's silver platter as he passed, "Oh, I wouldn't be looking for that to happen any time soon." She squirmed.

Her cousins had been friendly but mystified. Sage couldn't explain herself and knew she could never readjust to their lifestyle. Peggy, just a bit out of step her whole life, never following the same rule book. She knew, as the only little red-head in the family she was given some latitude for her rebellious ways—summers sleeping in her backyard tent, her collection of turtles and frogs, biking to school instead of riding in her friend's convertible, her choice to go to Oberlin instead of Duke, the family legacy. Now, everyone seemed to think she should grow up and return to the fold.

"Grandmother left you a brass trunk Peg, here's the key, even our parents don't know what's inside. The rest of us cousins already chose something from her estate, but she insisted this was yours. Open it."

Dragging the chest into the adjacent den, Sage retreated. "Think I'll haul it out of the way, who knows what ghosts lurk." She closed the door and tossing a pillow on the floor sat in her accustomed cross-legged position. She ran her hand over the chest's clawed animal feet and the hammered brass detail. In her memory, the small trunk had only existed as an end table to hold Granddaddy's candy jar. She'd never considered its contents. Turning the key and lifting the lid, Sage dipped her nose into the chest to smell the aroma of time—musty but fragrant from the wood lining the interior.

Why this chest and why for her, she wondered? Inside was a stack of rectangular, black-leather photo albums. Sage lifted them out one-by-one, each layer a different era of her grandmother's life. The deckle-edge photos were mounted on black pages by white triangular corners. Handwritten silver inscriptions meticulously documented happy moments from her grandmother Margaret's life.

The top album was filled with images she recognized—Peggy and her cousins at the beach, Christmas, graduations and weddings. The second and third albums in the chest regressed to the years with Sage's parents, her aunt and uncle, and earlier years with Granddaddy, great-aunts and great-grandparents. Margaret waving from their first automobile; Margaret posing in jodhpurs and boots; Margaret leaning into her husband in a white ruffled dress, tugging his tie and looking up in alluring submission.

"OK, Grandmother, why give these to me? To show me what a nice orderly life I'm missing? No scrapbooks of me with pictures of domestic bliss. If you only could see, my life is orderly and colorful and full of faces I love—the little girl who guides the flock of ducks to the fields in the morning; the ancient altars and mossy Buddha sculptures peeking from gardens; the glorious wedding of my dance teacher; the handmade patterns of the batiks, so valued in the world of fashion and decorating. I carry these images with me, wherever I go, Grandmother."

Under the well-ordered albums was a pile of old newspapers, bold, significant headlines from past decades: "Lindberg Lands in Paris," "U.S. Declares War-1500 dead in Hawaii," "It's Over in Europe."

Lifting away folded stacks of newsprint, Sage removed the last item hiding below the newspaper headlines—a smaller, older album. Decaying bits of black leather crumbled as she lifted it from the chest. Gently turning back the fragile cover to the first page, Sage was surprised to see an oversized professional photo of a young woman. A bold, dark-haired model in her stage costume; a skimpy burlap dress, fringed and ragged, slightly off shoulder and held coquettishly above the knee. Her waist-length hair draped over creamy young shoulders.

Grandmother, Margaret! I recognize you, but exactly which you is this? Your bold stare, the way you point your toe and hold your skirt? I can just imagine you tossing your hair and daring the viewer to ever forget you, Sage thought.

She flipped through pages of photos, one more surprising than the other. Featured on a page by itself was a stage bill from the Shubert Theater dated June 10, 1924.

Hoochie-Coochie Girls, A Musical in Three Acts
A newspaper clipping of a theatre review followed:
Lead actress injured. Understudy, Margaret Shannon, glorious replacement, a success!

Sage fingered the ticket stubs, fragile yellow Western Union telegrams of congratulations, newspaper write-ups about parties and galas from the society pages, pressed flowers and silk bows. Her mind scuttled over the dates, calculating her grandmother's age as twenty-two, and considered the era. The Roaring 20's, in New York City, Margaret was a *Hoochie-Coochie girl* on Broadway? "How did you keep this a secret, Grandmother?" Sage tried to read between the lines, to see the unwritten, the un-photographed; to imagine the unspoken stories of a life her grandmother had never shared.

Margaret
The dressing room off the main stage of the 44th Street theater was littered with flimsy costumes, feathers, tap shoes, net stockings—all lightly dusted with powdery make-up hastily applied. It was Margaret's third night as the lead, following the sudden departure of the star. Center stage, her dream come true after years of dancing and modeling and following her passion despite all her sacrifices and family objections. She had arrived. She read the congratulatory telegrams:

New star is born! stop So proud of you my darling stop Champagne this evening?

Long-legged red head storms the stage stop

Congratulations on your successful appearance in Hoochie-Coochie Girls stop

Margaret twisted the diamond engagement ring on her finger. She marveled at how much her life had changed and imagined her promising future. She shook off the memories of home—her father who had abandoned them; her mother struggling with two daughters, one hopelessly involved with the speakeasy crowd, and Margaret, herself, a runaway to the big city lights.

Her mother's words were still there to haunt her. "A working daughter, an *actress,* how can I explain this? Where will you live in New York? We don't have any people there. Praise God your grandmother isn't alive."

"Times have changed, Mother. It's my dream; New York has so many opportunities. I'm sorry, Ma, I'm going. I'll be safe at the Genial Women's Boarding house."

Margaret looked in the mirror and adjusted her oriental robe that had slipped off her shoulder and reached for the silver hairbrush with her future initials engraved on the back. "MDP" Margaret DuPont, a gift from her fiancé, a scandalous presumptive engraving as their wedding date had yet to be set. But he'd said he adored her and her waist length auburn hair, wavy from being twisted high on her head, when it hung loose like a long red curtain over her back. So many of her fellow actresses were bobbing their hair in the flapper style, but she knew her long curls and that color were two of the hooks all her admirers loved.

"More fan mail, Miss Shannon." The stage manager dropped another telegram on her vanity. Carefully protecting her manicure, she inserted an Emery board into the envelope, broke the seal and pulled out the telegram that *would* change her life, forever.

Mother very ill   stop   Return home immediately   stop   Your loving sister.

Sage

Sage shifted on the pillow and re-examined the telegrams, trying to determine who'd sent them. Who would have called her grandmother, "darling"? That was long before she'd met Granddaddy. In photographs, Sage studied her grandmother's hands—the way her fingers fluttered in front of her expressive eyes, wide and alert, how her fingers deliberately plucked the fabric of her shawl, how her toes pointed. Sage recognized the familiar gestures and exaggerated expressions in her grandmother's poses—surprise, coquettishness, alarm. They were not unlike her own well-practiced gestures in Balinese dance.

Falling from the last pages of the album was an unmounted telegram in its original envelope. Sage bit her lip as she read it and imagined the sharp disappointment her grandmother must have experienced receiving the command to return home. The album ended there. The remaining black, blank pages were left unfilled—no more playbills, no more pictures, no more pressed flowers.

Margaret

Margaret handed the porter her suitcases, hat box and valise, gave the conductor her Washington ticket, and tucked her return ticket safely inside her handbag.

Her most recent tickets had been round-trips to Wilmington, paid for by her fiancée. He'd met her at the station, top down on his Duesenberg roadster. When they'd reached the roads approaching his country estate, he'd let her drive. She had loved the feeling of independence, the power of speed as the road rushed by, her red hair whipping outside her scarf.

Their romance began while she was still a chorus dancer. She remembered the burning sensation she felt as his glance went straight from her red hair down to her long legs. She'd been the only dancer in the dressing room to receive flowers after every show. He'd been so proud of her new role at the Shubert, although *Hoochie-Coochie Girls* was a bit risqué, they both saw it as a stepping stone to further success. They had loved dancing together at parties, where she'd practiced all the etiquette and formalities required to calm his family's concern about her theatrical life. Even gone so far as to wash her hair in front of his mother to guarantee she wasn't one of those loose women who used hair dye, one of those flappers. Marriage into this family might cramp her independence, she'd thought, but he was sweet and attentive, and they loved their NY life together. And it was a promise of security and status beyond even her own high expectations.

Surely, I will return for the fall season at the Shubert and our New York social life. She knew he would never leave the City. Margaret double-checked her return ticket in her handbag and clutched it to her chest refusing to look back as the train left the station. She closed her eyes and took a deep breath listening to the train hiss and pull away. It had taken so much sacrifice and dedication to get here.

Sage

From her pillow on the floor, Sage leaned back against the wall, pulled her knees to her chest, and looked around at the room—the place she knew reflected her grandparents' long life together—art deco lamps, bookshelves, paintings, and oriental rugs. Her head felt heavy, dizzy with a new understanding of the woman she had felt so apart from, her namesake, the woman whose hair and figure she had inherited—her grandmother. Were they really so different? What if Margaret hadn't come home and met Granddaddy? What if she'd stayed in New York and married the admirer who called her, "darling"?

Why tell me? And why tell me now, Grandmother?

Preparing to close the chest, Sage saw a sheet of Margaret's monogramed stationary, a note in her grandmother's shaky script written in her signature fountain pen ink, dated only a few days before her death.

My Dearest Sage,

This box of memories is my gift to you. As you can see, there was a time in my life when I followed an unconventional, unexplored path to pursue my dreams and hunger for dance and adventure.

Don't misunderstand me, I have loved my wonderful husband, our life, our family. But there was always the door to my passion that circumstances closed. I may have tried to guide you to a traditional life, in part because I was afraid you would be hurt. But, dearest, keep your doorways open, follow your wildest dreams and passion, and know you come by your bravery and boldness honestly, just like your red hair and freckles.

Your loving Grandmother

Sage rose up from the pillow and pushed aside the gold brocade den curtain that covered the floor-to-ceiling window. Her little nieces were running in the manicured summer grass below, squealing and laughing. Her family could live their lives the way they pleased, and now she freely would live hers, she thought.

She selected the outrageous photo of her grandmother in her gauzy Broadway costume from the album and slipped it into the deep pocket of her batik pants where she'd kept her return ticket close. Touching the limp note to her heart, Sage let out the breath she'd been holding, mourning the grandmother she'd never really known, and thanking the grandmother who had cleared her road home.

Hard-Earned Wisdoms

Oh those intense crystal-clear horrible
Earth-and-psyche-shattering times
When our worlds tumble like crazy
Split apart
  and we dissolve
Fall apart   then
Gather up our warrior selves
  and strength
Come out whole
  and shiny new
With old wisdoms.

Ginny Daly

What We Steal

Sarah Barnett

Scene I. Sunday afternoon, Junior's restaurant. My family at lunch. Aunt Lee, who has an eye for fine things, says, "Aren't these the cutest salt and pepper shakers?" Mom, nods, looks around the room—families conversing, silverware clattering, waiters carrying trays of desserts topped with whipped cream.

My father glares. "Don't you dare," he says.

Mom's eyes widen to say, "Who, me?"

Scene II. Ladies' room. Mom opens her purse a crack, lets me peek at the salt and pepper shakers. If people hi-fived in those days, that's what we would have done.

My mother pinched coffee carafes from diners, soft blue blankets from United Airlines, a tiny silver bell from St Mary's hospital in West Palm Beach. The bell sits on my desk reminding me that crime sometimes does pay, if you count tschaschkes. I believe she thought she was giving her stolen treasures a better home.

We all steal something. I appropriate words, phrases, sentences. We call them writing prompts, but still… I lift these pieces as casually as Mom would sweep a small china pitcher into her handbag.

She fancied blue glass. I relish oxymoronic phrases—silent applause, jovial melancholy, deadly serious jest.

I wonder: Is this any different from pocketing a scalloped shell or multicolored stone from the beach? Aren't these scraps from novels, poems, magazine articles and ads just lying out in the open begging for rescue to a safe place on a windowsill or shelf?

Today I read this in the *New Yorker*: "My sweetheart, I had the vilest of trips." I don't care about the rest of the letter from Vladimir Nabokov to his wife, Vera; I've got a story started in my head. Maybe you have one too. A perfect writing prompt. If someone accuses me of stealing words, I'll defend myself with, "I'm giving them a better home."

Parkland in February

A woman waits in the doorway,
and maybe she is holding a dish cloth or
maybe she is holding a book or
maybe she is holding a baby or
maybe she is holding a paintbrush.

She is waiting.
She knows this is the time
   to wait, the time
the bus rounds the corner.
She knows she doesn't have to wait,
because he is big enough
to walk home from the bus stop on his own,
big enough to carry a cell phone,
big enough to make his own after-school snack.

But she waits anyway
because there is beauty in the waiting,
there is hope in the waiting,
there is that feeling in the waiting
she cannot name, that is all mixed up
with the scent on his pillow, the grass
stains on his soccer ball, the way his voice
makes "mom" into two syllables.
She waits, and in the tree in the yard
a woodpecker taps at the bark,
a fox squirrel clambers up the tallest branch,
the sun stripes it just the way it does
every day at this time.
She knows the time without looking at a clock.

She could go back into the kitchen,
on to the back porch,
into the basement,
up to the attic, even
next door where her neighbor promised her

Black-eyed Susans she can transplant in her garden.
She knows this, but she waits
because it is her waiting time.

Today there are few cars on the street,
and the bus is late.
She frowns.
The clock ticks on the mantel
in the living room behind her.
She had been listening to the radio earlier
but turned it off two hours ago.
She likes the soft silence of the house
in the afternoon.

She waits in the doorway longer
than she ever does, because the bus
is always here by now.

When the phone rings,
she knows.

She drops the dish cloth,
the book,
the paintbrush.
She holds tighter to the baby.

A single cloud passes over the yard,
and even the fox squirrel stops
chattering, just
for a second.

Ellen Collins

Another History of Childbirth

Judy Wood

The year is 1913 and behind closed doors my grandmother lies curled up with her knees pressing as close to her chin as her enlarged middle will allow. The light in the room is dim since the curtains have been drawn against the last rays of sunshine as it nears the dinner hour. The midwife moistens a cloth in the basin on the table next to the bed and gently wipes away the sweat that has gathered on her patient's face. Low groans emit into the room and it is hard to tell which of the women they are coming from as their heads are bent so close together.

The men closeted together outside the birthing room listen to the radio, smoke and drink coffee that costs about a nickel a cup. The endless puffs from their cigarettes fill the air. Last year they were listening to this same radio as the announcer gasped the news that the Titanic had gone down. This year Al Jolson is singing his new hit, "You Made Me Love You." They are a gruff but friendly bunch varying in age. Most are farmers with rough hands and sturdy bodies tanned from the many hours spent working in the hot sun. Straw hats and overalls are the fashion statement of the day. Chickens strut and peck in the yard and occasionally, when a stray gets a bit too brave and pushes its way into the room, one of the men grabs it and tosses it out again. Over the hours of waiting, the milkman and the mailman have been the only visitors.

My grandmother is stoic and pleased to be able to get through this birthing experience here in her own room in her own way. If things go wrong, the doctor will be called. He would very likely have pushed the midwife aside and, using forceps, pulled that baby, my mother, out into the world. Or maybe she would have had to be heavily medicated and her little one would have arrived sleepy, most probably with breathing problems and the need to be resuscitated.

A new drug called "twilight sleep" that makes you forget the pain had recently been discovered and was being used by wealthy women. Grandma could not have afforded it and wouldn't have chosen it anyway. She knew about the labor required to have a baby. She had watched her sisters and listened carefully to her mother's stories and her grandmother's before that and was well acquainted with what to expect. She came from tough New England stock and wouldn't have blinked if she had delivered this baby out amongst the blueberry bushes, scooped her up and walked back up to the farmhouse to put dinner on the table for the very same men that now wait outside her door.

By the time I was born in 1948, many positive changes had been made to the childbirth experience. More and more women were having their babies in hospitals. Physicians had mostly replaced midwives although this was a controversial part of the new day. Still a woman's experience depended on her status and her ability to pay for the more modern techniques and equipment. My mother's description of her ordeal suggests that her own progress was limited. As she told it, she had laid in a cavernous room side by side with many other women in cots resembling cribs with high iron rails that were cold to the touch and so many of the women did not have pain medication and the noise level from the screaming was intense and the doctors were late and the nurses were busy and the women that had received the "twilight sleep" weren't sure what was happening and where they were and the whole experience seemed to leave them all with the sense that they were floating outside of their bodies and suspended in real and yet unreal time. The story always made me groan and pray for more progress by the time it was my turn.

Thankfully, by the time my own daughter was born in 1977, women were on a roll. The National Women's Convention propelled the rights of women onto the world stage and there was no turning back except by their own choice, in childbirth. Women were reconsidering the use of midwives. Home births too were popular again. Squatting births either at home or in hospital and water births grew in number. Great thought was given as to whether or not to opt for all-natural childbirth or to call the anesthesiologist. Not being a stoic like my grandmother, I was more than pleased to be able to choose to have an epidural. Pain? No thank you. My daughter, however, uncooperative from the start, was in a hurry to arrive. Did it hurt? Yes. Did I hold it against her? Maybe.

I did enjoy the luxury of a semi-private room and the ability to draw the curtain and allow myself some privacy. I had a nurse to wheel me into a spanking clean delivery room where my very familiar and comforting OB/GYN would arrive at my side to deliver my baby. Husbands were now allowed in the delivery room. A great addition to the process? Hard to say. The Bee Gees latest hit song was "How Deep is Your Love" and in that room on that day before the epidural kicked in, I wasn't exactly sure.

My daughter had her daughter in 2008. Women again had made great bounds historically. Hillary ran for President and although she lost, she did allow that now "there are 18 million cracks in that highest and hardest glass ceiling." And new mothers were certainly no longer sheltered behind closed doors. In fact, those doors were flung open before the new mom had caught her breath ushering in hordes of family and even a few close friends who would exclaim, laugh, cry, pinch, kiss and hug until finally someone would smartly suggest that perhaps it was time to let the new mom get some rest and everyone would surge toward the door and bustle out again.

A hundred years ago, doctors could only gather info about a baby's progress by listening through a stethoscope. The array of choices we have today is so broad as to be confusing. Scheduling the date you prefer to have your baby is now so popular that 30% of moms choose to be induced. Discovering the sex of your baby is possible now too and is a subject debated enthusiastically often over a cup of coffee that might now cost as much as $5. It is hard to predict the future for childbirth and progress in women's rights. I saw a cartoon in New Yorker magazine this week. One woman said to the other: "in a former life, I was exactly the same."

Supper

On a small Chesapeake Island
In the damp gloom of an October night
My hungry weary soul stands before what
Is the season of waiting and
An open fridge with a portion of cabbage,
Two limp spring onions, a pliable carrot, one garlic
Clove, a leftover leg of some poor skinny bird
Brunello uncorked, of course I raise the chalice of my life,
An etched shapely wine glass that is a legacy
Of my courageous grandmother,
Zita Philomena Cahill O'Rourke
I coax the carrot into
Icy water revival
The green onions also have a come to Jesus moment
In their own baptism
This, the twentieth hour of the day, I summon
The Spirit of the evening to bring on the wisdom hours
And I say
For God's sake where is the *Bouquet Garni?*

Jane O'Rourke Bender (October 2015)

Published posthumously for Jane O'Rourke Bender,
August 4, 1946-September 25, 2016.

Mary Woodwell Corbett Fowler

From Indian Captive to Foremother of a Nation

Mary Leach

The Kidnapping

On April 22, 1746, in the Massachusetts Bay Colony Settlement IV, later named Hopkinton, New Hampshire, a raiding party of Abenaki Indians kidnapped sixteen-year-old Mary Woodwell along with her parents, two brothers and three other men. There had been reports of 'savages' in the neighborhood, so Mr. Woodwell, a leading citizen of the small community, ordered his family and a few hired men to hide in the garrison he had built on the edge of his farm. According to Mary's account of her Indian captivity dictated decades later, the Woodwells weren't that concerned initially; relations between the settlers and the Indians were pretty good, with the Woodwells careful to respect their neighbors. The Abenaki and other Algonquin tribes in the region, their numbers decimated by disease, were more likely to carry out attacks on one another than on well-armed and well-fortified British settlers. In particular, *Pennos,* leader of the local tribe, was well-known to the Woodwells and according to various accounts had 'received numerous kindnesses from the Woodwell family'.

The French and Indian War

But far from little Hopkinton another war was brewing: the major fight over territory in the Old and New Worlds that ultimately involved much of Europe and became known as the Seven Years War. Today in the United States we term the part of the war that extended throughout the colonies, but primarily involved New England, New York, the Ohio Valley and Eastern Canada, the French and Indian War.

Before the 'official' outbreak in 1756 of what would become in effect a world war, there were many skirmishes throughout the colonies. Both George Washington and Aaron Burr—later considered hero and traitor respectively—led colonial battalions in that war. But fighting was especially fierce along the borders of settlement outposts in the New World. Both the French settlers in Quebec and the New Englanders in New Hampshire, Massachusetts and Connecticut cultivated Indian allies.

Although the tribesmen and the settlers murdered one another, the Indians valued living captives—especially British captives—more than scalps. These captives could be sold to other tribes as slave labor and to the French for goods and currency. The Europeans in turn could then hold their captives for ransom or for trading with the enemy's captives.

Indian Captivity Narratives

Hundreds of Indian captivity narratives like Mary's can be found in various historical societies, including the one in Hopkinton. While life in captivity was clearly challenging, the Indians fed, clothed and housed their captives and, in particular, did not rape female captives. Mary recounts that the squaw to whom she was initially traded used her primarily for agricultural work. That she was treated reasonably well she attributed to Pennos, who had personally interceded on her behalf.

However, that she was treated well was not unique to her situation. In another Captivity account, that of a British settler who gave birth to a daughter during the actual kidnapping, her Indian captors provided privacy during her labor, herbal medicine to ease her birth pains, native clothing for the infant, and a horse to ride on as her husband walked alongside. In contrast, Mary's mother, Mary Carril Woodwell, also captured in that Indian raid of 1746, had been immediately transferred to the French. There is a legend that she had tried to stab her captor with his own knife. She died of yellow fever in a prison in Quebec that same year. There was no herbal medicine for her!

According to her narrative Mary spent about three years with the Indians, then was transferred to Quebec where she was held for another six months until being ransomed in 1750. The details of the ransom are sketchy and somewhat contradictory, perhaps befitting the memory of the 93-year-old Mary. In one version, it is the Dutch who ransom her alongside various Dutch captives; in another it is her father who has expended his health and nearly all of his fortune in attempting her rescue. In that account, her rescue involves some trickery. A local doctor is said to have given Mary something to make her appear near death, thus persuading her Indian captor to release her to the French to avoid bringing that sickness to the tribe.

Life after Mary's Release

What is documented is that Mary returned to her father's farm. There she met and married Jesse Corbett and gave birth to Josiah and another son also known as Jesse. A few years later Jesse senior died by drowning in the river—circumstances surrounding the drowning not specified, and Mary married again, this time to a Jeremiah Fowler with whom she had five more children.

According to her unnamed chronicler, Mary died in Canterbury, New Hampshire, a town adjacent to Hopkinton, in 1823 at the ripe old age of 93. Her son Josiah, born in 1758, and according to the *National Archives Records and Administration US Revolutionary War Roles, 1775-1783* databases, served as a corporal in the American Revolution. Josiah married Elizabeth Lankester, and they had several children including the third Jesse Corbett.

The Shaker Connection

That Jesse and Elizabeth had children was indeed fortunate since in 1792, Mother Ann, the founder of the Shaker movement with its pacifist philosophy and insistence on celibacy, came to New Hampshire. Shaker communities formed in both Canterbury and Enfield, neighboring villages of Hopkinton. Perhaps influenced by the border skirmishes of his childhood in the 1750s and 60s and the carnage of the Revolutionary War, Josiah and his wife became members of the Enfield Shaker community and are buried in unmarked graves in the Shaker cemetery. In keeping with Shaker principles that disavowed marriage, Elizabeth is recorded under her maiden name and buried as Josiah's sister.

Hopkinton, which for a time was actually the State Capital of New Hampshire, although it quickly ceded that role to Concord, is still a small rural village, albeit one with a very active historical society. Enfield houses a well-regarded Shaker Museum with many buildings and artifacts from the original community.

Birth of a Nation

During Mary's remarkable 93-year life span the United States of America came into existence. At her own birth and throughout her captivity she would have been firmly British; indeed, she and the other Congregationalist members of those tiny settlements feared the wicked—and Catholic—French, whom the British outnumbered, historians estimate, by some twenty to one. She would surely have been delighted when in 1759 the British General James Wolfe roundly defeated the Marquis de Montcalm at the Plains of Abraham leading to the surrender of that same Quebec where she had been held as a hostage.

Fifteen or so years later she could have decamped with many other 'Tory Loyalists' to Canada when those hotheaded colonials in Boston declared war on the British. Instead she saw her first born, a member of one of those 'well-regulated militias' later celebrated in the Second Amendment of the U.S. Constitution, fight those Redcoats in the American War of Independence.

In her old age she would have witnessed what we now call the War of 1812 where Britain reasserted its military might and held the upstart nation to its current borders with Canada. She saw what had been part of a Massachusetts territory emerge as a state in its own right, and she lived through the presidencies of Washington, Adams, Jefferson, Madison and Monroe. While it is unlikely that she could have foreseen the infant nation torn apart by a horrendous civil war over slavery—slaves were rare in the New England colonies—she would almost certainly have adopted as her own the famous New Hampshire motto "Don't Tread on Me' now frequently cited as the banner for State's Rights. Or perhaps, given her lived experience, she might have preferred the motto found even today on New Hampshire's license plates, "Live Free or Die."

Midwives and Foremothers

There is an extensive body of academic literature about women who were held as Native American (Indian) captives, but they are little celebrated in popular culture. When we envision colonial women, we are far more likely to imagine them elaborately costumed and dancing with gallant British officers than tending fields, slopping hogs and doing the gritty, backbreaking and often dangerous work that life in remote outposts required. We know that Mary gave birth to seven living children in conditions that appear truly horrendous to the modern eye. She may well have endured many other pregnancies, since infant deaths were common, and she probably would have aided other women in similar circumstances.

While presidential wives have been identified as 'Foremothers'—Martha Washington, Abigail Adams and Dolley Madison are particularly celebrated—surely women like Mary Woodwell Corbett Fowler deserve special recognition as well. If it were not for their bravery, their willingness to endure and indeed surmount what are almost unbelievable challenges, would the hotheads who planned the American Revolution have succeeded in their endeavor? Thomas Jefferson may have forgotten women when he penned that famous declaration that "All men are created equal." Abigail Adams may have reminded her husband John to "Remember the Ladies," but it took over 130 years from the founding of the Republic to guarantee women the right to vote. With all respect to their more storied sisters, it can be said without exaggeration that Mary and those like her are also the foremothers and midwives to the birth of the nation. Without their willingness to sacrifice would there be a United States of America today?

A Personal Note

I'm a mongrel, my forbears the 'wretched refuse of your teeming shores.' My paternal grandparents and maternal great grandparents fled poverty, disease and civil war in Ireland and came to America in steerage—some sneaked in through Canada—to take up menial occupations in the slums of Boston and New York. For me, genealogy was *Trivial Pursuit*, very suitable for retired academics like my spouse who can trace his lineage back to the founding of Maryland and the *Ark and the Dove*, but not very interesting to me. That all changed, however, when I learned a few genealogical techniques and, in the process, discovered that Mary Woodwell Corbett Fowler is my great-great-great-great-great-great-grandmother and Josiah the Revolutionary War corporal turned pacifist Shaker my five-times great grandfather.

While I don't think that genealogy will ever cure cancer or eliminate world hunger, and while I believe that what you make of your life is far more important than who your ancestors were or what they accomplished, I have learned a great deal through this excursion into my past. At the very least I now know that I probably inherited some of Mary's Yankee stubbornness!

When the Universe Opens

You have to stand in stillness sometimes,
listening to the tissue paper rustling of grass,
the moon-drawn music of the tides,
the muffled pace of low clouds
bringing in a storm.
Lift your hand in the air
and see how that gull far out over the water
seems perched on your fingers just for an instant,
as if the two of you share the ecstasy of flight.

The white bird becomes a speck over the horizon
as you look down at your feet in the silken water.

You have to stand in stillness sometimes,
where for a silvered moment
the grass
and the tides
and the clouds
and the wings
gather you
in.

Ellen Collins

This poem was first published in *The Memory Thief* in 2015.

She writes and writes
because the stories won't stop
      because writing is her way of dancing
    it is how she keeps breathing

The Snow Party

I met him the winter of 1964,
at a snow party.
If you're from New England
or Minnesota or anywhere
north of the Mason-Dixon Line
you're allowed to smirk
that six inches of snow
cancelled classes
at the University of Maryland
where I went to school

and no classes was the perfect
excuse for a fraternity party.
In the basement
of the Theta Chi House
I nursed a Coke in a plastic cup
and waited for a ride back
to my dorm.   What was I doing here
in my prim Tartan plaid box-pleated skirt,
matching V-neck sweater
knee socks and penny loafers?

A non-drinking prude,
I sat alone in a corner
on a lumpy threadbare sofa
and watched beer slide over
the hands of partiers and slosh
onto an already sticky tiled floor
as hips swiveled and twisted
to a recording of James Brown
coarsely pleading
Please   please   please
baby   don't go.

By spring the frat boy and I were lovers
parked in his new blue Mustang
in a space in front of my dorm,
the windows cranked down
to let in a breeze carrying
the scent of newly mown grass
as we breathlessly fumbled
with buttons and zippers
keeping an eye out for
passersby and watching the car clock
to make certain I got to the front door
in time for curfew.

Now, over fifty years later,
we watch together as the snow
drifts around the base
of the Weber Grill
on our deck and sprays
of flakes like powdered sugar
stick to the windows.
We sit by a fire
sharing the Sunday *Times*.
Mozart fills the room
as I ease down
into a leather Stressless chair
and   silently wonder
whatever became of those
two   wild college kids?

Judy Catterton

Marina's Wish

Terri Clifton

Marina frowned at the line of cars on the Avenue, stretching as far as she could see, like all the days of summer elongated before her. Today had been blistering hot. The concrete beneath her feet radiated heat.

Summer had barely started but already the town was packed to its gills with tourists. No parking was left, and every seat in every restaurant was occupied. Waiting lines flowed out onto the sidewalks. Music played, horns honked, and a remarkably loud child cried.

She stepped over a melted ice cream cone, longing for escape, unable to take the clamor any longer, making her way down to the now nearly deserted sand. The boardwalk ran parallel to her escape, but she looked away, let her gaze slide east, out over the open Atlantic, ignoring the red ball of sun easing down behind the resort town.

This edge of the sea was the only place she could find enough space from the crush of summer chaos. Eventually the boardwalk ended, but she kept journeying on, past luxurious homes, not caring how far she'd gone, seeking refuge. Onward still, she crossed beneath the shadow cast by one of the concrete watch towers, looking up at the landmark that had stood guard since WWII. Alone at last she sank to the sand, inhaling as deeply as possible, salt air clearing her lungs of the man-made taint of creosote and car exhaust.

A pod of dolphins slipped south, blue-gray bodies rolling effortlessly between air and sea, reflections of the last sunrays burst on their wet skin, gone when they submerged again. She wanted with all her heart an existence as serene, thinking only beautiful thoughts. No clocks, no conflicts. Dolphins were smarter than humans, she decided, as they moved out of sight. If she'd been born a mermaid she'd have followed. Trade this difficult human world for an ocean life.

Darkness was falling. There'd be no escape tonight. She stood to go home, lingering when she noticed a glow of imminent moonrise, the first full one of the season.

The emergent rounded edge tossed diamonds. The light skipped across the water, ending where the waves touched the shore, retreating when waves took the magic with them. The rippling light looked like a path and she laughed, imagining that she could just walk to the moon.

Perfect in its roundness, the orb continued up, and she walked closer, meeting the gentle wavelets, advancing and receding, leaving her feet to sink as the waves pulled away. Music floated to her, she thought from the town. The melody was beguiling, and she listened to catch the lyrics. Impossibly, she thought, it was coming from across the water. Curious and needing to hear, she lifted her sundress above her knees. The water felt cool, soothing her as it swirled about her tanned legs. She could hear a woman's voice now and pieces of a refrain. Part of her was sure she knew the words, had known them all her life, could remember them if she could just get closer. She half believed she really could take that path of moonlight and keep going, to wherever the singer was. It lured her deeper.

The water reached her knees, her hips, her chest. At first she didn't notice the lack of buoyancy, that her feet stayed firmly on the ocean floor as she walked toward the sphere on the horizon, only a heaviness lifting away. It was odd that as her head slipped beneath the surface her feet never lifted from the sand, and she might have been afraid if the singing hadn't suddenly become louder. She never stopped to wonder why she didn't need to breathe.

Above her, moonlight poured down, penetrating the dark water. She could see clearly. Her attention was caught by a school of shimmering silver fish. Moving as one, a million tiny bodies spiraled, surrounding her, then with a last reflective flash, were gone. She tilted her head back to watch them swim high above her.

The singing stopped as a woman suddenly appeared. Hair of the darkest blue-black billowed around her like a storm cloud. Her eyes were the clearest blue. A circlet of gold and coral glittered. She held a trident spear.

"Be quick!" she said. "You must repeat your wish before the moon reaches its zenith."

"My wish?" Marina was confounded by her presence, confused by her words. "I never…" She must be hallucinating. Had she drowned?

"The one you spoke to the moon."

"No, I—"

"You did!" The spear pointed at Marina's chest.

With the sharp tines only inches away, she tried to remember. "I did…I wished…I wished I was a mermaid." But that had only been inside her head hadn't it? Had she said it aloud?

"Granted!" The woman tilted the trident back and tapped the handle three times on the sand. A dull booming echoed around them.

Marina looked at her sundress floating around her, at her feet on the sandy bottom, searching for something reasonable or rational. "But I don't have a tail."

The woman shrugged. "You weren't born with one. You may grow one in time."

The idea was absurd. "Who are you?"

"I am Nerissa, Queen of All the Seas. I have granted your heart's desire, and your soul is now bound to the water." She turned away, all interest gone.

"Wait! What am I supposed to do?"

"Do?" Nerissa frowned. "I care not."

Nerissa had shimmered and broken apart, disappearing exactly like the school of fish.

Marina considered this world of various shades of blue and black, wondering again what she was supposed to do. Lacking an answer, she was left to look for one, and over the next days and weeks—never needing to sleep—she searched. When she discovered mountains that rose from the seafloor to dizzying heights she swam up to stand on top of them. She delved underwater caves, and great deep holes that didn't seem to have a bottom, spent hours playing in towering forests of kelp. She swam with dolphins, finding she was faster than before, fins or not. And early on she'd made a friend, if one could ever call a mermaid a friend.

The singing had started again after Nerissa had vanished, softer and closer than before. Swimming in a moonbeam next to her was a proper mermaid. The moonlight shimmered on scales of deepest teal as she danced in the light, and her long hair flowed, silver white. Marina was surprised to find her tiny, the size of a young girl, and that her smile revealed a row of shiny, pointed teeth.

When the mermaid touched her bare chest, pointing to herself with a graceful wave of her hand, her name popped into Marina's head as if she'd always known it. In all the months she'd spend with Xyla, she never would hear her speak, only sing. The important things were simply impressed on Marina's mind, invading it in one-word bursts. "Eat," when she'd shoved the oyster at her. "Danger," when she'd yanked her hair, and dove behind the rocks. But her song was the single most beautiful thing Marina had ever heard.

Every month, when the waxing moon pulled at the tides, she would crave oysters and Xyla would lead her to the beds. Prying the shells open with a dagger she'd taken from a shipwreck, she'd swallow the slippery insides, pearls and all. In fact, it seemed that more and more it was the pearls themselves she craved. Satiated, they would swim to the surface and slip onto the rocks to lie for hours under the moon. A longing to sing would rise up in her, an overload of beauty, and she'd wish she could release it the way Xyla could.

She didn't notice the increasing luminescence of her skin until one full moon night when she shined brighter than the sand she lounged on. It wasn't many moons later that she noticed the first scale, a dark lavender, set like a jewel on her ankle, but she still didn't sing.

There was other music in the ocean almost as beautiful as the siren's song. The happy sing-song of dolphins she'd follow into shallow crystal water, the closest she let herself to the daylight and the powerful sun. She swam there less and less with time, drawn to the darker blue coldness and the dreaminess of whale song. But her favorite was the opus of storms, breaking against a rocky coast in a symphony. Safe below, she'd venture close to the collision, let the deep bass rumble and roar.

She'd been over and around every sort of shipwreck. Wooden ships, skeletal and disappearing bit by bit. Metal ones that held their shape and were filled with life. She'd seen coral growing from a chandelier, and touched the bannister of a once-grand staircase. The sands at the bottom of the ocean held treasure from teacups to gold. Rings and coins. Chests and bottles. And bones. She would always slip by those, refusing to think further about the beings they had been. So at night she lounged on the bottom, just letting the roar fill her, and the objects came floating down from above, she knew what was happening. There was a boat captured by the storm, breaking on the rocks. She looked over at Xyla who had just caught something shiny in her hand and was examining it with a distant curiosity. Whatever it was, she dropped it to the sand, and held out her hand to catch another.

There would be people in the water as well as things. "We have to save them," she said, but Xyla's black eyes were devoid of concern as they shifted upwards. Marina didn't bother to repeat herself.

The looming black rocks were threatening. Wind and currents created a violent pull. Jagged boulders could split hulls or smash a skull. She'd grown strong with seasons of swimming, but the power of the ocean was immense and tireless. All her new strength might count for nothing.

Just below the surface floated a man. Pushing him, she rose up through the churning and into the air. Waves peaked and sloshed all around them. She held his head above water until she could pull him ashore on a stretch of sand.

She looked at him. He was painfully young, not a line on his slowly bluing face. She rolled him over and pushed against his back, forcing out as much water as she could, but he didn't stir. Turning him back, she lowered her mouth to cover his. As her lips met his cold ones she realized she had no breath to give him. She wanted desperately to fill her lungs, to force his open. Desperation made her try again to compress his chest, willing him to breathe as she pumped. When he choked, she turned him on his side, letting him retch. She envied every ragged intake of air that rattled inside him. Once he stopped coughing she put her head against his chest, needing to hear a heartbeat. She saw a flashlight bobbing in her direction, heard voices. Rescuers. She touched his face and his eyes fluttered open, just for a moment. Living eyes. She slipped back into water.

Below the surface she went, swimming fast and deep, shaken from her complacency. When you cry at the bottom of the sea there is no difference between the ocean and your tears. They are meaningless. Apathy is not peace, she understood now. Being human and alive meant a whole spectrum of things to feel. Deaden one emotion and you deaden them all. How had she wished away her own life so easily? Her teardrops were only water mingling about her.

Nerissa arrived with the force of a depth charge and a boom, echoes of which resounded and rolled like thunder. "You had no right!" Octopus ink flowed from her hair. Her eyes were ice.

"He was dying."

"He was mine! Everything, everything, in this water belongs to me!"

Marina tried to swirl the ink away. It was making her mind fuzzy and she shook her head.

Nerissa moved, changing form, something dark that Marina couldn't quite make out. "I gave you what you wanted."

"Well, I don't want it anymore."

One black tentacle slithered across Marina's foot and she watched it wrap around her leg. Despite the sting, she didn't flinch when Nerissa ripped away her single purple scale. Blood looks like smoke in the water, she thought, as a wisp left her ankle.

Later she would attribute her prescience, her moment of clarity when she knew exactly what was coming next, to instinct. She wouldn't remember the single, insistent word in her head—Up!

She pushed hard from the bottom in the instant before Nerissa launched the trident. It missed hitting her, but the action stripped her of whatever she'd been turned into that first night in the moonlight. She kicked hard for the surface not knowing how far above that actually was.

Her lungs burned but she held on, knowing that to give in would mean her death. It would be her bones that would whiten in the sand. When the water around her started to seem brighter she knew she was either dying or very close to life.

   Her head broke through into a summer night. She gasped, gulping precious air, treading water and letting oxygen spread through her. She smelled land. Waves were breaking on a shore. She turned.

   The moon hung full and low in the west, setting over the dunes. Its diamond shine once more lighting a path, this time to take her home. She swam with energy and purpose, but no fear, reaching the beach as night gave way to a new morning, emerging once more into her messy, chaotic, irreplaceable human life.

Dancing Queen

We are always the same age inside—Gertrude Stein

In flannels and fuzzy socks, I pranced
around the living room, pretending
to be the Dancing Queen, young and sweet,
only seventeen, as my baby slept
and my remote spouse changed channels
in the den. It was Friday night, lights
were low, but there was no place to go,
and so I danced alone, tripping
over sippy cups and stuffed bears.
How I wanted to reclaim those nights
in fevered fern bars, where they played
the right music, stiletto heels clicking
on polished floors, synthetic skirts
swishing to the beat. I could dance,
I could jive, I could have the time
of my life. Now, I seek serenity
savasana's static pose, inner peace
on the churchyard labyrinth. Yet…
when the music plays, my body strains
to recall, revive the old moves. I want
to be the Dancing Queen, still
having the time of my life.

Irene Fick

This poem was published in Irene Fick's new chapbook, *The Wild Side of the Window* (July 2018).

Dancing in the Venetian Rain

Kimberly Blanch

Venice caught in a warm, sweet-tempered rain possesses a theatrical quality, one that is inclusive of those who find themselves scampering towards the next shelter and those who are more daring who saunter, enjoying their moment of fame on the cobblestone stage.

Since arriving in this enchanted city, I've often heeded the call to quietly wander through the twisting, turning alleys with gates, doors and shutters sealed so tightly that nothing could find its way in, not even a lonely, wayward raindrop. However, on one particular night, I made the acquaintance of quiet's long lost relative, unbounded joy. Absolute euphoria she has been called by those so deeply moved by her.

The music coming from the sound-amplifying buds nestled in my ears filled my heart and set fire to my soul. An impulse ignited a place within me like a spark setting dry kindling ablaze. I couldn't escape it. It begged me not to run from it but, instead, to move with it.

"Dance," it whispered seductively. "Let me weave my way through you. Heed me." Such a persistent proposal it offered. Any resistance I returned was politely refused. Why not take a chance, I asked myself? Who would see me and who would care? Was anyone even out here in this late summer storm?

A key I had forgotten I possessed opened a door within me. My knees softened, my feet un-weighted themselves from the stones beneath them. The rain was coming down with perfect timing, like a movie scene designed with precision. The puddles held within the well-worn curves of the ancient stones offered exclamation points to my footfalls, expressing excitement for the incoming tide that was taking hold of me.

The umbrella's curved handle began to swing within my grasp. As I felt my fingers loosen their hold, a nudge of encouragement from my wrist coaxed out a grander swing and the sweet rain found my face as the umbrella resigned from its customary position and became my prop.

The droplets of rain lit me up, as if they fed the fire. Is that possible, water feeding fire? Clarity came. The elements had their own agreement and their symbiosis had been fueled.

My body melted into the melody. My steps lengthened. I got out of the way and my soul took the wheel. Over bridge after bridge I took flight and floated, touching down only to launch again. Spinning and swirling. All of me was alight. Was I Debbie Reynolds, Gene Kelly or an alchemy of the two?

Singing along, I sensed the vibrations within my vocal cords. And as my awareness caught their effects rippling through my body, I felt them shake loose the fibers that had been held with such intensity for too many years. I could not recall a time in my adult life when I had moved so freely, so unhindered. Without contraction, without shame, without judgment. And here I was, so seemingly conspicuous, yet so invisible.

The song played on, the lyrics evoking within me a desire to maintain this flame. *Why let it end,* whispered my heart. I felt an aliveness that had been dormant far too long. This was living, pure and raw. And how soulfully satisfying it proved to be.

Each corner provided options. Where was I? And why did it matter? How I longed to know these alleys and where they took me. In time…in time. Just enjoy getting lost for now, I decided.

The Bridge of the Barefoot, *il Ponte degli Scalzi*, stood like a stage showcased by the lights of the Santa Lucia train station. The beat of the music continued to drive my feet, up two steps, down three. A sweet little swirl and back up three steps. Reveling in the momentum, the mental snapshots clicked at a rapid-fire pace. Capturing every step, every spin, every swing of the umbrella as I made the melodious journey over the passageway upon which the barefoot monks wandered for more than three hundred years. It was that smooth-trodden Istrian stone that held my last remaining dance card that evening. So sweetly it waltzed me towards my home, humming the last few bars with me and bidding me golden dreams in its native tongue….*sogni d'oro, carissima!*

Exhaustion found me as my fingers lingered on the cool, slick stone railing. I knew it was time to point towards home. Class came early. And that's what brought me here, this lilting, lyrical language. How I craved it. Having once dreamt in Italian years ago, I had often found myself willing it back to me. To think, to feel, to breathe, to speak, to write in this language was what brought me here.

And *here* I was….to dream again.

Lessons Learned: Taking Care of Myself

Lisa Graff

My mother had never called my college dorm. Long distance was too expensive. Her voice sounded foreign when she said, "I'm sorry, honey, but we just don't have the money to send you back next year."

It was March 1973 and I was nearing the end of my freshman year at Frostburg State. A year fraught with anxiety and excitement, this freshman had achieved a 3.6 and was the happiest I had ever been in my life.

Only a month ago my boyfriend, a handsome corpsman in the Navy, had asked me to marry him. We had looked at pots and pans and had driven to Colorado to meet his parents. He said, "I'll always love you." But I said, "Then you must wait. I have to get my degree."

When the call ended with my mother, I thought about returning home. My father's drinking was out of control and they argued all the time. Our house was not a happy place, but in the mountains, in my room and on campus, I had made a new life and was immersed in World Literature, Oral Communications classes, and Psychology 101.

That evening I wrote a letter to my state senator asking for a scholarship. Always the child my family labeled melodramatic, I can still remember my tears made the ink run on the stationary.

Then I mentioned my plight to the RA, the resident assistant, and she informed me that I could apply to become an RA, too. She said the job paid room and board, and that was all I needed to hear to complete an application.

A few weeks later, a girl I knew down the hall came to me crying and asked if she could talk to me. In the confines of my room, she said, "I think I'm pregnant and I don't know what to do." I knew there was a counseling center on campus and offered to go with her to see if she could be seen. They spoke with her that very night.

I had many papers due and classes to attend and threw myself into my studies. In late April, I found out I had made the initial cut of applicants and would be granted an interview. And on that same day, I learned that my boyfriend had magically found solace in the arms of one of my high school classmates. Guess I made the correct choice.

While I was nervous, I was determined to stay calm on the day of the interview. Applicants were told we would participate in a role play. An RA would pretend to be a student with a problem and come to me for advice on what to do.

The actor RA sat down beside me and said, "I think I am pregnant. What should I do?"

I almost started laughing which would have cost me dearly. I believe things happen for a reason. That sometimes we are given help through destiny or a Supreme Being. Here was evidence that a power greater than myself might be at work in my life.

"You can go to the crisis center on campus," I assured her. "They know what to do and say. I can come with you."

I got a call back for the final interview too. In May I learned that I got the three-year position, and I ran to tell the RA on my floor. She congratulated me and said, "That's impressive for a freshman. Well, I guess you don't have to leave college."

"Well, at least not for one more year," I sighed.

"What do you mean one more year? The RA job is yours until graduation once you get it."

I began to cry. Three years of room and board paid for! Really? I knew I could come up with the tuition money somehow.

She looked at the tears on my face. "Well, they will take it away from you if you really mess up." We both began to laugh then.

That summer I found a waitressing job, which was demanding and exhausting, but it paid well. I saved every nickel. I would lay out my tips on the table in the kitchen and my father would watch me count the money, his cigarette smoke spiraling into the air. I could tell he was proud of me although he never said so.

Then in mid-summer, I received a letter granting me a senatorial scholarship award, an amount enough to cover tuition costs for the next three years. I dropped to my knees in gratitude. It seemed like a miracle now—my college degree would become a reality. I would be the first one in the history of my family to obtain a four-year degree!

When I graduated in 1976, my family came to watch me receive a diploma. My mother gave me a book of Robert Frost's poetry. Together we had recited "Two roads diverged in wood" once when I was home on spring break. "Two roads diverged in wood, and I chose the path less traveled."

The path less traveled was the path to a college degree. A degree which led to a teaching job and then a career. I loved teaching then and still do now.

I took charge of my destiny at the age of nineteen. Even though now I am happily married, I never expected someone else to take care of me. I can take care of myself. That lesson is the most important one to learn in life.

A Cougar at the Starboard, Dewey Beach, Delaware

Nancy Powichroski Sherman

You know you shouldn't accept a third Tanqueray & tonic, but you're enjoying the attentions of this sexy lifeguard. Andy. Even his name is cute. So what, if this beach boy is at least ten years younger than you? All the better that *he* doesn't seem to notice. You revel in this feeling of *college girl* even though you're long past your sorority days. This is what you had hoped would happen on this weekend at the beach—this time away from the job hunt, the family responsibilities, and the monotony of monogamy, a.k.a. your marriage to Ted.

You only half-wish that Fran had stayed at the Starboard with you. Sure, this weekend hasn't been great so far, but this is supposed to be a reunion. Has it really been fourteen years since you and she were roommates at American University? You can't believe that time has rushed through your life with the speed that your son Max used to tear down the hallway to escape a bath when he was a toddler. But fourteen years? You do the math. Max was born almost a year after graduation, and he just turned thirteen in April. My God! Sometimes you forget, or at least you try to forget, that you're the mother of a teenager.

You wish that you hadn't thought of Max just now. What would your son think of you if he knew that Mom is weighing her morals vs. her needs? And at this moment, your needs are the larger of the two. You and Ted are having problems, as the cliché goes. Ted's been distant, and you've been distant, and maybe the distance this weekend might be the cure. Or maybe not. This weekend in Dewey Beach, Delaware, will be the litmus test.

You hadn't heard from Fran in years, though you'd occasionally run into her mom at the mall: "Franchesca is doing so well…. Franchesca got promoted to the international office…. Franchesca is in Europe this month…. Franchesca's Philadelphia home is being showcased in *Architectural Digest.*" Okay, maybe you'd made up that last one. But your ultimate defense of "Really, Mrs. Whooton? So, Frannie is still single?" ended her litany every time.

You laugh. Beach boy asks you what's funny. You tell him some crude joke that you heard Ted tell his brother last week—the one about the virgin, the farmer, and the horse. He can't hear the punch line over the music. You repeat it louder: "That's not my horse!" You both laugh.

There was a horse on the front of the Christmas card that Fran sent you this past December, the first card in years. Its postscript of "Miss You" opened the door again between you and her. When had that door been closed anyway? Was it your excursion into mommy-hood or Fran's into the world of textiles? When had the birthday cards stopped and the last phone calls been made?

You were glad that Fran had suggested a get-together for this May weekend at Dewey Beach where you and she had spent that infamous week after graduation—that week when the Delta Gammas had the entire second floor of the Dewey Beach Motor Inn—that week of parties and guys and barhopping and, for you, a magical night at the Starboard when a handsome fisherman showed you fireworks on the beach.

Beach boy puts his arm around your waist, drinks to your eyes. *His* are milk chocolate—so are his shoulders which jut out beyond the frayed edge of the cotton shirt, the sleeves cut away just for this effect. Oh, to be twenty-one again, you might wish, but really, you're glad to be past all those insecurities. Back then, you would have pictured yourself married to beach boy. Now, you just picture yourself naked with him. But it's just a game, and you're enjoying it.

When you had mentioned the reunion at the beach to your husband, he said, "You and Fran in Dewey again? Sure. Go. Have fun. Just remember that you're married and stay away from the Starboard." So, if anyone is to blame for your spending this time with beach boy, it's Ted. Stay away from the Starboard? No effing way.

Beach boy leans over and kisses you behind the ear and tells you that you're his kind of woman. You look around at the girls on the dance floor and think, *does that make me a brainless beach bunny?* But you smile and tell him what he wants to hear—how handsome he is, how marvelous his physique is, how you just love a man who saves lives. A part of you hopes he'll save yours this evening, if having a wild night of crazy sex can perform that miracle. You blush at the boldness of this thought. Realize that the game is getting more dangerous than you'd planned. Are you really considering doing the dirty deed with this kid?

Beach boy Andy rubs your back in a circular motion. A "hmm," almost a "yum," slides from your mouth. You can't remember the last time that someone rubbed your back.

You glance at the clock above the bar—11:53 p.m. You hope that beach boy will make his move soon. Before you chicken out. Before your makeup gets stale and lets those worry lines creep through. Before your tight black dress wilts and you with it.

A busty cheerleader-type keeps brushing up against him as she reaches for bar pretzels. You wonder if her boobs are real, or if she'll ever face losing one of them like you almost did last year. No, yours are originals with only a tiny biopsy scar on the left one, a reminder of how close you came to the disease that had killed your mother. For a moment, you hate this girl. You hate that she's pretty and that she's young. You hate that she's the right age for beach boy. You hate yourself for sitting in this bar and pretending to be what you're not.

You never told Fran about that scary time facing breast cancer, and you don't want to think about now it, either. Think instead of the last time the two of you stayed here in Dewey, the afternoon you sat in room 211 painting your nails pink like all the Delta Gammas and planning how you'd live in France, meet important men and marry them, and be movers and shakers in the fashion industry. Those were great days.

It brings a smile to your face. Beach boy thinks the smile is for him. You don't tell him the truth. Why start now? "Are you having a good time?" he asks and laughs. It seems an odd question until you realize that you've been keeping time to the music with your hips and he's been enjoying the show. You work your hips some more, this time with a come-and-get-it wink. You think of *Sex and the City* and wonder if you're trying too hard.

"Having a good time. Wish you were here," echoes through your mind. It's what Fran had written on the postcards that you and she sent each other during that last vacation together—free ones from the front desk—a photographic collage of the front of the motel, the pool, the inside of a room, the ocean, and the words "Dewey Beach Motor Inn" in gold italics. You still have the card. You saw it when you were looking for your old bikini to pack for this weekend. It's in your lingerie chest at home, a piece of tape holding it together where you'd torn it in half—you don't remember why. It sits there with the lace teddies and the thongs and the old diaphragm and the expired box of condoms, all just part of your scrapbook of useless items that drawer has become.

You take stock of the lingerie you're wearing tonight. Black plunge bra. High-cut matching panties. Acceptable, but lacking any real pizzazz. When had you stopped buying designer lace and started buying Walmart?

For the last month, almost daily, you had pictured this reunion of you and Fran. Tanning at the beach. Munching Grotto pizza. Drinking and dancing here at the Starboard. Scoring some guys. Playing them like you did fourteen years ago—a game that Fran called stupid when you mentioned it to her during dinner a few hours ago.

You remember how Fran had given you hell that night of senior week when you left the Starboard to walk the beach with the cute fisherman who'd been buying you "college girl drinks" at the bar. You remember accusing Fran of just being jealous because she hadn't scored that night. The next morning, the two of you would make up. She swears that she was only trying to be protective; you maintain that you were only trying to be your own person. It was the moment when you drew the line of demarcation between the safety within sorority walls and the great unknown of post-graduate life.

You wonder if Fran is still in the motel room, or has she driven down to Bethany Beach looking for a piano bar and a glass of wine? That's how you picture her now. You can see her sitting alone at a table, leaning back into the curve of the chair, her legs crossed, her right hand displaying the wine glass in the air like liquid berries. She'd be dressed in summer classic style. Probably a Lilly Pulitzer sundress and Tori Burch sandals. You think of how she looks like her mother—how her clothing is coordinated to the nines, how she wears her blonde ponytail tied with grosgrain ribbon.

You think of that afternoon at the beach, you in the bikini you hadn't worn since before you got pregnant, and Fran in a one-piece Tommy Bahama. You on a beach towel, and Fran under an umbrella. It was like you and Fran were on different vacations together, or like you were at the beach with Mrs. Whooton. She/Fran/Mrs. Whooton looked at you over her Maui Jim sunglasses; she looked like a freakin' *Vogue* cover. She told you she's engaged—finally and for the first time—and she wanted to tell you here in Dewey.

Engaged?

And he's a VP of something or other. You didn't listen after "VP." What mattered to you was the realization that she had it all—once again, just like in college—the looks, the money, the success, and the guy. What mattered to you was that you no longer had the card to trump her mother's hand. You felt resentful of so many things: Of how Fran was invited to pledge the Delta Gammas before you. Of how her parents took her to Europe every summer and invited you to tag along as her guest. Of how she lived the dream that the two of you had shared on that afternoon of painting finger nails and giggling about meeting the right men and building your careers.

"I want you to be my Matron of Honor, of course."

Matron? The word stops you. You cringe.

Beach boy thinks you're chilly. He puts his arm around you. He blames the air conditioner nearest the bar. He suggests you and he leave and take a walk on the beach. "We can look at the ocean," he purrs. He runs the side of his left hand along your thigh, and it seems so obvious, but feels so sexy. He pulls you closer, between his knees on the barstool. He kisses your mouth. You taste the warmth of the whiskey on his lips and inhale the fragrance of his skin, the hot smell of musk and sweat. The scent touches some ancient part of your memory. You think, "Screw her and her wedding plans. Screw her and her Delta Gamma pink fingernails." In your mind, you substitute "look at the ocean" with "screw," and tell beach boy that you'd "love to."

He guides you down Saulsbury Road. The heat you feel isn't diminished by the ocean breeze. Neither of you talk. You let him lead the way. You're committed to doing this—no turning back now. Still, you wonder if your underwear is pretty enough and if the night is dark enough to hide the flaws. Your chest flutters as you wonder whether he has a condom with him. You wish that you'd been smart enough to have taken care of this yourself. Did you learn nothing from the last time you walked this beach with a guy, the fisherman, fourteen years ago? You should have packed a condom in your purse just in case, but you didn't know that you would do more than flirt at the Starboard tonight.

Beach boy stops near a lifeguard chair. You figure that it might be the one where he sits during his day job. He leans you against the wood frame and gives you a passionate kiss, pushing his body tightly against yours, letting you know that he's ready for you. You feel a rush of excitement and crazy scared at the same time.

Your mind flashes to a wedding. Fran in a Carolyn Herrera gown. Flowers everywhere. Fran's dad walking her down the aisle. *Your* dad didn't walk you down an aisle. *Your* parents weren't going to plan a wedding in which you would wobble past their family and friends in a gown meant to camouflage the "bun in your oven." *Your* dad gave Ted directions to the Justice of the Peace and a warning that he'd better provide for you, and treat you well, and raise the child you and he had made that night on the beach. Max.

Before it can begin, just as beach boy starts to run his hand under the bottom hem of your dress, everything collapses. The game. The plan.

You push him away and fall apart, tears pouring out no matter how much the timing is wrong.

It confuses beach boy. "What's wrong?" he asks.

You tell him that you've walked this beach before. You tell him that you made a baby. You tell him about Max and Ted and your marriage. The words spill all over the place.

Beach boy changes his approach. He says it's okay, holds your chin in his hand like you've seen in some made-for-television movie on the Hallmark channel. He invites you back to his place where he promises to make everything all better.

For over a month, you dreamed of this night and how it would make you feel. You were wrong. Fran traveled the world and met her important man, and Fran doesn't need a Dewey lifeguard, and this guy is more a jackass than a find, and the feeling is wrong now, and you know that the tears aren't about the past, aren't about the night you tore the postcard, the night that Fran accused you of settling, or that you believed her. The tears are for yourself. For how easily you could have broken a vow. How much you could have hurt your son. How cheaply you were willing to give up your honor. And for what? To get even with Fran? You were never on an even playing field, so how could you return to a nonexistent place?

So, you say, "*The fault, Dear Brutus, is not in our stars but in ourselves.*"

He looks confused. It doesn't compute. Why would it? Who quotes Shakespeare on the beach in Dewey where they'd gone to get laid?

"My name's Andy," he says.

And you say, "It doesn't matter."

Beach Boy may not have read *Julius Caesar,* but he's smart enough to realize that he's not getting any tonight, and that he's wasted three Tanqueray & tonics on you. Suddenly, you've become some loony tune to him. He calls you, "Nut case!"

But it doesn't sting. It doesn't matter. *He* doesn't matter. He feels played, like he's played so many girls. You guess that he's not used to being played, especially by a cougar he'd found sitting alone at the bar.

You walk away like you could have when you were twenty-one. Except that, if you had, then there wouldn't be a Max, and you would never have known that tiny little baby's entrance into the world, or his first steps, or Little League, or his recent crush on a girl in his math class. And deep down, you know that Ted loves you. And really, you love him, too. It's just been a bit of a bad patch, that's all. Blame it on Fran's Christmas card. Blame it on second guesses. Blame it on your cancer scare. Just a scare, but it was enough to want to turn back time and start over.

Ring Fran's cell phone. Say, "Matron of Honor calling." Ask her if she'd like some pizza with an old friend to celebrate the upcoming nuptials. While you wait outside of Grotto Pizza for her, phone Ted and say, "Having a good time. Wish you were here," and mean it.

First published in Nancy Sherman's book of short stories, *Sandy Shorts*, published by Cat and Mouse Press, 2014.

She writes to celebrate
        and to mourn
She will not be silenced

Waiting for Sunrise

Barefoot guests tiptoed
on sand cooled by the night
murmuring *finally   finally*

orange and red flaming lanterns
lofted into the dark sky
seagulls chanted
waves whispered prayers for the sun

the minister in black robe brought
her wife and the singer
his husband

a black dog and a man watched
from a distance
the circle of friends closed in

brides linked hands
walked silently to the shore
silhouettes
against a veil of grey marble clouds

on cue at 6:04 vows spoken
rings exchanged
the sea opened her arms
lifted the veil

and the sun
sang Hallelujah
to the new day
and to the lovers

who had waited so long

Sherri Wright

In celebration of the wedding of Jane Klein and Sherri Swenson "Waiting for Sunrise" was first published in *Letters from Camp Rehoboth* in November 2013.

How to Fall in Love with a Woman

Become a Hospice volunteer while married to your husband and raising three sons
Move from Kentucky to Virginia and begin your first job since your children were born when your youngest is six years old
Become a discharge planner in a rehab center
Change jobs after nine years
Begin working with a new Director of Rehab
Attend all meetings with this woman regarding discharging her rehab patients
Develop a friendship with her based on a shared philosophy of treating patients with dignity and respect
Have a boss who shares none of these values
Begin walking four miles a day after work to safely discuss work issues
Laugh a lot
Learn a lot
Share a love of nature and animals
Appreciate her inner child
Have her partner fall in love with someone else and move out
Be a friend as she grieves the loss of her relationship
Do a masterful job of consoling her
Notice when her white Ford Explorer is at work
Wonder why you care whether her car is at work
Realize that life is not as joyful or interesting when she is away
Find her still at work at 8 p.m. when you leave the room of a dying patient being taken off life support
Appreciate her loyal and loving character
Be unable to eat or sleep
Accept that you love her
Tell her
Accept that she loves you
Be told by your husband that you can never see or talk to her again

Leave your husband and hurt the family you have loved and protected for thirty years
Learn about the greys in life and lose some of the black and whites
Hire a lawyer and wait four years for your husband to agree to the divorce
Wait seven years for your two younger sons to speak to you
Live with the consequences of your actions
Be grateful that enough time passes that you are forgiven by your family
Be humbled that your new paradigm means loving and accepting all people, not just the people who were in your small box
Walk out onto the damp sand at sunrise with close friends and marry her on her sixtieth birthday
Be grateful for every moment of the nearly twenty years you have had together, as you are told she has a brain tumor
Struggle to breathe and support her going through chemotherapy and radiation
Struggle to watch her endure unbearable pain and loss of independence
Be the caregiver you never expected to be, and keep her at home
Absorb and rejoice that your sons and grandchildren grieve for her as family
Be thankful for your supportive friends who remain at your side
Cry with her and for her as Hospice is called in to control her pain
Hold her hand as she is released from her pain and eventually lets go
Be overwhelmed with loss but cherish the loving memories that will sustain you
Live with the consequences of loss
Forever

Jane Klein

Dedicated to Sherri Swenson, August 3, 1953-May 12, 2016.

She and I

Jane Klein

She was 5' 6 ½ inches tall, and whenever anyone asked her what she was up to, she replied "5' 6 ½." I never remember her missing this reply to the question. I am 5'8" tall and never thought of that reply, though I think of my wife whenever the question is posed to me. It is funny how little things stay with you about someone you cared about.

She found it impossible to disengage from a conversation with anyone, no matter how late it would make her to the next appointment with someone else. I would be so anxious to be on time to meet her that I would put my coat on to leave even if someone were in my office talking about work. I was out the door, only to get to my destination and wait for nearly an hour, because she was asked a question by someone on her staff as she was leaving her office.

She was unable to sit through any movie that had violence or strong emotional content. She left a movie that won an academy award because there was child abuse in the storyline, and our friends had to drive me home. I can't say I enjoy movies with violence either, but I enjoy some movies other than Disney animated films.

She was a vegetarian and had been since college, while in my house which included my husband and three growing boys, being vegetarian was never discussed. When she and I lived together, we did eat vegetarian at home, since in my opinion, it was not worth the effort to make a separate meal after a long day at work. I became so accustomed to it that I would frequently forget to order meat even when eating out. Alone, I rarely go to the meat counter, though going to burger night is now a Monday night ritual.

She was left-handed, and I am right-handed. My father was also left-handed, but I could read his writing, which was not always true with hers. She had her Masters in Physical Therapy and had been the director of her department since the age of twenty-eight, but they did not teach grammar in her early years in Ohio. Neither she nor her brother had ever met a comma, and I often teased her that someone else must have helped her with papers in college. Our "Christmas Letter" was a nightmare to edit, but she was the one who maintained connections with grade school, high school, and college friends. I have a few contacts from a distance, but she flew to Nevada most years to meet with the friends she made in her first two years of college, and she always remembered their birthdays.

She never had any children, while I spent my adult life raising three sons. Our past several years before meeting were entirely different, but she was naturally more attuned to our nieces, nephews, and grandchildren than I could ever be, though they all knew they were loved. I remember looking out the window of our house in Virginia and seeing her with my granddaughter when she was three, both covered in leaves, their laughter so robust that I could hear them through the glass.

If I had to describe her in one word, it would be *authentic*. She had wash and wear, salt and pepper curly hair, usually kept short, and needed no make up. She tanned in five minutes due to her olive complexion. I burn in five minutes, have never been tan, and have fine, straight hair. I have been known to joke that the closest I could get to having a tan and curly hair was to marry her.

She could be showered, dressed, and out the door in ten minutes. I need forty-five minutes to add make-up and do anything tolerable with my hair, the true color of which I haven't seen in thirty years.

She was a fitness devotee for many years, either running or riding her bike in good weather or reading work related books at 5 a.m. while on her Nordic Track in the winter. I join gyms, walk, and even did spinning for a few years but not with the discipline she had. She took no vacations from her exercise routine, running or using the gyms wherever she stayed. She found out all about the area she was visiting from her runs, while I was in our hotel room with my Starbucks.

She never missed one day of work for any reason in twenty-two years while director of her department. No matter the weather nor how she felt, she made it to work in her white Ford Explorer. I, on the other hand, would definitely take the snow days and maybe an occasional mental health day when appropriate. Of course, staying home on snow days meant I had the shoveling job, so she may have been on to something.

She had known she was gay since she was a teenager but didn't tell her parents until she was twenty-eight. They were very conservative, and she feared her father would send the men in the white coats to come pick her up and take her to a clinic for "repair." I had never once thought of women in that way until I was fifty-one and fell in love with her. My parents were both deceased by then, so I never had to struggle with the guilt of disappointing them in addition to my husband and three sons.

She had a brilliant, impish inner child that I coveted, and I am more of an old soul. She was afraid of very little while I am afraid of everything, though I am the one left behind to finish life without her. Our spirits were in tune with respect for people, animals, nature, and love.

The main difference now is that *she was,* and *I am.*

Dedicated to Sherri Swenson (August 3, 1953-May 12, 2016).

"She and I" is based on an experimental essay structure taught by Maribeth Fischer in a class titled, "Experiments in Writing," Rehoboth Beach Writers' Guild, 2018.

She's Come Undone

Everyone has that freedom inside
locked away deep
so you'll never find
That freedom you try but
just can't justify the way you feel
It's two sides to you it's true
but the freedom that's inside of you
Too huge to push away
Away the urge to just release
and be who you will be
Ahhh… This magical feeling
This joy I'm feeling
It's good for me
It's so good for me
FREEDOM!
It entertains me
and always relates to me
I just can't shake it
it's urging me to let it out
but I'm scared it's much
Too much pressure for me
Can't sleep, I'm feeding on it
Wish to get lost in this
Too good to be revealed in its
Finest state
Ohhh… This escape
who dares to debate
I love who she's becoming
Love how she's looking now
how she's talking now
Best of all what she's thinking now
Thoughts she never thought possible
Filled up with so much bliss
not allowed to let it out
But it's calling me
It indulges me

Needing me to just oblige it
in this task, this journey
I call unity with the natural and spiritual worlds
What can I say in adornment
At a feeling, this utopic finding
That somehow makes so much sense to me
And I bet it would do the same for you
If we all were free enough
To let it out
Only breathing, only alive
when bits of you are released
You are the very rhythm of
my beat
With each sway of my hips
Giving away the fragrance of
Your liberty
Whenever it seems you're
fading out
through this guise of life
You reappear greater than before
leaving me in the most lustful state
one can imagine
You pleasure me
You arouse me
You send me
To heights never surfaced before
Hit depths too deep to translate into words
At times feeling so surreal to this whole idea
Must remain connected to you
You keep me composed
just thinking of how good it will be the next time we meet
So please
don't take so much time to
come back to me
I've waited so long to find you
approach you
Now embracing you
like nothing I've ever known before
I moan passionate purrs of seduction in your presence
You and I are meant to be one
Much more than
a form of chemistry

This here is destiny
Manifesting itself in the more
Exotic tone
My world away from this world
My escape route and haven
when things get too tight
You make everything all right
for me
You literally turn darkness
into days
Days where sunshine comes from my insides
and expose futuristic views of
you and me
We are what's left
for the world to see
Now come to me
and taste a sip of harmony
Let me give to you
what nothing on Earth
can buy you
no amount of luck could grant you
Now close your eyes with me
and visualize life's finest views
Mmmm...
Intoxicating you are to me
I'm all loosened up
My soul is free
for once I can let my guard down
And just be Me
I wish to drown in this
Somehow learning of elevated
dimensions in you
in order to somehow
Grow closer to you
become more of a part of you
Through your lens I see
Realms yet to be mentioned
Ever spoken of
I want to be re-grounded in you
creating some grade 'A' foundation
Deposit into me
the answers of life to come

I desire to be impregnated by you
Impart your glorious philosophies into me
The open vessel
For you to be revamped through
Store your legacy in me
I will surely die like this
but I'm always alive with this
I'm realizing
You are too big to fit on my paper
As my thoughts of you continue to protrude my mind
My hand won't write fast enough
Too little ink to fill my pen
Penmanship not neat enough
To attempt to describe you
What a fool I must be
to try and confine you
I must set You free!
Allow you to exist in the imaginings of minds
who only dream of having you
all figured out
There are too many levels of you
and although I may never
see them all
I need to exist in you
Thinking of ways
Ideas of how to make an adequate description of you
How to explain your whispers
in the air of all who inhale
Yet and still I sit here
Pen in hand
Persistent on having ink droppings spell words in your favor
Hoping all who hear me
have the chance to experience
a moment in You!

Ash'iz "Tha Rebirth"

Death

I will die in a daughter's nondescript guest room
in a rented hospital bed
on a blustery autumn day
sometime after my eighty-eighth birthday

Another daughter will attend to my nursing needs
although she has not been a practicing nurse for many years now
and the third daughter will be concentrating on what loss means
this time
in this place
as she begins to make arrangements
for what will happen once my spirit has departed
its confinement

That's the daughter I told years ago
to just burn my body to a fine ash
and distribute it in their gardens
these three daughters and my son

And they will all say
Mimi Dupont has died
no one but them knowing
that the IRS knows me by another name
and come spring my ashes will be dispersed like seed in the wind
among four gardens
and my headstone
will be a short stick
among the others
radishes, spinach, lettuce, Mimi

Mimi S Dupont

Freedom Yearning

I was not born to be forced. I will breathe after my own fashion. Let us see who is the strongest.
    —Henry David Thoreau, *On the Duty of Civil Disobedience*

Mid-sixties high-time Berkeley, reverenced now by culture cool adolescents; flower-power, wilted into this century's pedaled lore. Still, this distinctive era, idol-held, holds something more:
Picture lava flows of candle drippings —soft cement formed hard— in nubby rug, hazard-laid, on darkened, dank, apartment floor. Window dressings —heavy bedspread covers— absorb party-crashing-eye-hurt-glare, keep shadow sure.
Gauzy blood-red scarves drape bubbling lamps, and incense, constant, holy-burns; its potent smoky blend a fragrant disguise, as intense unbeaten-bongo-silence sets this scented scene.

Imagine walks toward lively campus, a straight-hiked-stretch along wired Telegraph Avenue.
Feel every passionate petting pause beneath the towering campanile, brief hesitations, always, for free-thinkers lost between classes, between loves.
Such studied embraces provide needed conformity, among these non-conformists, offer imitated bits of joy and supply mimicked stony gladness on faces framed by Cody's student-store; international fare, if nothing more....

Listen as free speech echoes, and strains of Shankar–Ravi's music-soothe spaced-out spirit.
Novel theories circle 'round these universal minds —sober, clear, or time-confused— their halos of protected innocence dull, obscure, but not yet lost.
Watch young scholars study peace; their peers, like slaves the century before, off to Canada's escape.

And here, where no prison-cell imprisons, student flower-power's passive civil disobedience arrives, to liberate free speech —and witness right-wing-paranoia explode!

Enemy and contraband appear everywhere —in establishment's bully-brute-minds.
Forced curfew demands its restrictive hold and confiscated mail peels open before Federal postal inspector's forever old ominous stare.
The governor orders public assembly to desist and cease, treats Berkeley's student flock as the criminals they are not!
Why Reagan, why? To safeguard what?

I often *float* back —to that unsafe, timely, awe-filled, time— to People's Park, formed through cause-demand, by pure and simple 'sit-down-revolt' cure, and remember the peaceful chants repeating, what's **right** and **fair** and **just**.
A coming of age free speech movement, here, with gentle people, *singing songs and carrying signs* —just good folk gathering, in protest against a bloody, unjust, war.
No guns, no shields, no bullets, or bombs, they're just brave, disarming students, who dare to use the turbulence of words to rattle the walls of time.

People's Park looks pleasant now, so manicured, so hauntingly civil-tame, the simple vintage pattern of peasant garb, once worn, returns, in memory of the park's acclaim.
The city's *tired, poor, huddled*-homeless-*masses*, now claim their humble bed-size-plot each passing night....
In a sudden flashback, I fear for their safety, recall the horror of brute patrols armed with teargas, bayonets, rifles filled with birdshot, then buckshot, bullets as they attacked student demonstrators.
Public peace gatherings, though banned, stood their ground as National Guard moved in, leered at the fear on student faces, and stormed through academic halls until dawn's gold staked its claim on each new day.
Could police again enforce a cursed curfew, bar laundromatic way —my dorm-dragged dirty wash, a humble burden, my wrinkled crime?
If the intellectual idealism of youth holds true establishment threat, does any threat seem real?

I remember to stop by Telegraph Repertory Cinema to honor student victim James Rector, his stomach blown apart by called-in-troops, ordered to seize the fenced-in-greens of People's Park that Bloody Thursday.

Worn-wise university steps accept my climb and haunting echoes guide my way;
I enter my old room through its unlocked door, glance out third-floor wall of glass, eye-catch the red-warning-signal-glare of Alcatraz.
Salty-tear-blurred eyes urge me to strain, relinquish long held, ghastly, images of my psychedelic '60s, battled black & blue.

The turbulent period, though ever-present in my mind, has passed....
While recalling what was, I take a drive, one Sunday, and, as San Quentin comes into view, I ask myself why human rights and social justice still elude our country's capacity to grasp?
I think of Bogart's Dark Passage, his clever coupe-escape;
Look detective-deep into nearby cars— what secrets lie exposed?
Familiar feelings recapture my white-knuckle fear; I deny their treacherous hold. Will time forgive my oft-repeated errors, purify all soul's stain?
Will I feel the scrupulosity of 50-year-old civil disobedience, now unframed, dissolve in simple Ruthless truth...?

This reverential haunting now completes itself.
This guided imagery, new-age set, invites my traveling mind's conscious return, from then to now, and seeks absolution's grace to relieve the guileless guilt these pain-filled, tumescent memories hold.

Establishment's vindictive blame and consequence taunts —haunting echoes of ancient 'call to action' cries— hurled at good-willed targets, soon elicited student activists' response;
They rallied, formed their ranks, served their purpose and heroically paid the era's demanded 'counter friction' cost.

Every passive launch-back to the balancing act of savage history's pages, uncovers possible revisionary steps for each new seeker, and, heartfelt forgiveness —the way to peace— ever so slowly ratcheted through years of prophet-hammer-screams, engages.
Hoisted by justice and trust, humility's burden becomes lighter, ever lighter, as hope restores itself.

And so, I share memories of 'my' 1960s, a tumultuous decade, lived, survived —idealized by those not part of what was then;
They were not there to witness the abomination's impact; they do not know; my words... cannot explain— not now....

This is not another hijinks-trip taken to recall the bold heroic decade,
 with its excessive exuberance, its will to overcome.
Like Thoreau, *I was not born to be forced. I will breathe after my own fashion* —for I have come to recognize, in truth, 'who is the strongest'.

Each generation carries with it the strength it needs to stand against the wrong it condemns; holds the courage to speak out against what is counter to its values; embodies the will to resist every action that interferes with our precious civil rights, and, has witnessed the raw determination which erupts as each citizen vows to protect freedom's *treasure* from coming, undone, undone, **undone**….

Ruth Wanberg-Alcorn

We Women of a Certain Age

walked boldly by men
at construction sites
who hooted and howled
cat-called and belched
lewd and lascivious at
we women of a certain age who

were expected to type and teach and mother
but not doctor, engineer, and pilot
we were given dolls and irons,
toy ovens and tea cups
not microscopes and go-karts

we women of a certain age
saw job ads that read *help wanted men*
and knew we were wanted only
in laundry rooms   not board rooms

employers asked
we women of a certain age
if we planned on having children
and when we said *yes* refused to hire us
we women of a certain age did find

jobs where we were expected
to get coffee   get mail
get pinched   get children
off to school and dinner on the table

we women of a certain age
had less clout   less pay   less respect
were shut out   shut down   shut up
were told *no you can't*

no   *you shouldn't*
no   *you won't*
no
but then
we women of a certain age

stood up
spoke out
and said
just watch us

Judy Catterton

Office Politics

Marjorie F. Weber

In a time when most women chose to be wives who stayed home with their children, we were "liberated," the first wave of women hired into corporations in the 1970's for jobs other than secretary, nurse, telephone operator, librarian or teacher. We were hired on temporary contracts to fill affirmative action quotas by managers who would rather have hired men if they could have, managers who called us "ladies," who expected us to fail and didn't hesitate to tell us.

We wore our hair cropped short in neat layers or blunt cuts and our make-up light—not too much lipstick (never red), a touch of mascara and eyeliner, never eye shadow. We spent our first paychecks on the uniform, classic suits with padded shoulders and clean, straight lines, suits by Evan Picone and Jones New York—black, navy, camel, gray, and in summer, bone and pastel linens, our attempt to blend in, to look more like the men we worked for. We added pale blouses and gold chains at the neck and pearl or gold hoop earrings and, underneath, we wore lace camisoles and satin panties to remind us we were women.

It didn't matter how foreign the work seemed with its unpronounceable technical terms, algorithms, and acronyms—CSS, TSS, TFS, POTS. It didn't matter how little we knew before we were hired. We learned it. Quickly. Or we disappeared.

In hermetically sealed offices, in 6x10 squares of fluorescent lit space, in the hush of white noise, we bent our heads over our papers until they told us we could break or go home. We forgot the feel of the summer sun on our faces, the leisure of lingering over a morning cup of coffee, the touch of a baby's cheek against our own.

In the offices of the men who managed us, we politely admired the rows of family pictures on their file cabinets, the pretty young wives sitting on the back deck of their half acre of heaven, gathering up their children in their arms and smiling up into the camera. We listened to stories about weekend barbecues and day trips to Long Beach Island and tried not to notice when a few of these same men kept us a little too long at a meeting or when their eyes strayed to the base of our throats, to our breasts, to our knees and primly crossed legs.

We left our pictures of husbands and lovers, daughters and sons in our wallets, showing them only when someone asked, which was rare, because that was the rule—"temps" didn't mix socially with permanent employees and women didn't talk about their families.

At lunch in the cafeteria, over tuna sandwiches and Diet Cokes, we celebrated our paychecks and the freedom it brought us and pretended. If we had children, we pretended that we hadn't dumped them in day care where strangers witnessed and we missed their first steps, their first words, their first friendships. If we were single, we pretended that this last break up meant nothing, that we hadn't wanted marriage and children anyway. If the husband was out of work again, we pretended that we didn't mind, that we were making enough to support the family on one paycheck.

Nights, we mothers collected our children from day care and served up dinner—spaghetti or meatloaf, whatever we had left in the fridge or, God knows, Cheerios, sometimes—and, after supper and baths, bleary-eyed, we played warden while they did homework, longing only for sleep-in time the next morning. Which we never got.

If we were single, we gathered Fridays after work at bars and clubs and singles get-togethers. We hid our loneliness behind casual smiles and danced to Donna Summer and Billy Joel and Van Morrison, sometimes hooking up but more often not.

We never talked about the downside, the days too filled with work and errands and chores, the days with not enough time for our children, our husbands, our lovers, ourselves. We never let on that this work we spent so much time doing was tedious or that, sometimes, we longed to have the lives of our mothers or sisters or best friends.

It was just temporary, we told ourselves, this upside-down life.

But it wasn't.

THIS IS FOR US
international women's day

i guess there is an international women's day
because we need a day to celebrate the genitals we were given
or the ones we chose
so happy women's day.
here's to the selfies when we feel pretty.
here's to getting paid what we deserve.
here's to farting,
snoring,
drooling.
eating the entire pizza by ourselves.
here's to paying our own checks.
here's to not owing we should choose to pay ours.
here's to selfies and here's to brains and
here's to knowing every boy band lyric and
here's to not smiling at every person you pass on the street and
here's to every man who tells you to smile also agreeing to pay your
    phone bill
because if we are dealing in unnecessary ridiculousness
then let's go the whole nine yards baby.
here's to too much to say and hoping i have enough lifetime to say it.
happy woman's day.
i experience this 365 times a year.
i hope you do too.
here's to the love i want to want and the tears i choose to shed
and the help i get to ask for
and the sweatpants and short skirts and the sex i say yes to
and the pizza i say yes to and the morning breath
and here's to me breaking in your arms
and here's to me finding solace by myself and...
here is to this day celebrating us.
here is to me praying that one day,

this day
will be
every
damn
day.
until then
i will offer all my pretty.
all my nasty.
and all my attitude,
while sobbing as i break apart in your arms.
and to you feeling the tears,
and not feeling like you need to save me.
happy day.
happy wednesday. or monday. happy day ending in "y."
happy women's day.
here's to one more day when i get to kick ass and no one says, that's good for a girl.
no it's good for me.
here's to today:
another day in all the years i get to celebrate being me.

Annie Plowman

Enfolded

I have never felt so much like a woman
I have never felt like such a woman
I have never felt so fully, wholly a woman

as when reading other women's words
folded in firmly but gently with my own

Mimi S Dupont

Author Biographies

Ruth Wanberg-Alcorn is a former teacher, children's librarian, correspondent and graduate student at UC Berkeley, in the late '60's. Mother of five, Ruth has also established several writing groups in NJ and MD and currently lives on Maryland's Eastern Shore.

Ashley Cuffee, aka Ash'iz "Tha Rebirth" uniquely mixes alternative health with spoken word poetry that revives, reveals, and brings a rebirthing that heals. Off stage, Ash'iz is an Alternative Health Crystal Practitioner and Executive Director of the non-profit Beauty 4rm *(pronounced, "from")* Ashiz Movement. Most recently, she published a poetic-autobiography entitled, *"A Piece of Me, Brings Peace to Me."* Ash'iz is currently working on a complementary monologue called "Invisible Me."

Sarah Barnett has had careers as a teacher, librarian and lawyer. Now retired, she lives in Rehoboth Beach, Delaware, where she writes essays and short fiction, serves as vice president of the Rehoboth Beach Writers' Guild, teaches writing classes and enjoys leading "free writes" for other writers. Her work has appeared in *Delaware Beach Life, Delmarva Review* and other publications.

Jane O'Rourke Bender, 8/4/46-9/25/2016. Jane retired to Tilghman Island, Maryland, after her retirement as a clinical social worker. She joined the Rehoboth Beach Writers' Guild and engaged in her lifelong love of poetry. In her poems, she eloquently shared her struggle with cancer, always with her signature wit, wisdom and grace; one of them was published posthumously in 2017 in *The Divine Feminine: An Anthology of Seaside Scribes.*

Kimberly Blanch has had the pleasure of membership in the Rehoboth Beach Writers' Guild and the incredible opportunity to be published in *The Divine Feminine: An Anthology of Seaside Scribes.* In addition to her interest in memoir, sunrises, and sunsets, her passion to serve the community holds a special place in her heart.

Christy Walker Briedis joined the Rehoboth Beach Writers' Guild after retiring from a successful retail career in Rehoboth Beach. Writing classes opened a new world of expression and offered a challenging way to satisfy her creative urge. Her first published story was in *The Divine Feminine: An Anthology of Seaside Scribes* in 2017. She enjoys telling a good tale at Rehoboth Beach Writers' Guild events—*Songs and Stories*, and *Art in the AM*. With a passion for nature, she splits her time between gardening in Rehoboth Beach, and skiing in Canada.

Cynthia Gratz Campbell is honored to have her first published essay in *She Writes: Visions and Voices of Seaside Scribes*. Her life and writing have been shaped by her two beautiful daughters. The oldest, Rose, 25, is challenged by autism. The youngest, Elena, now 20, joined the family from Russia, at the age of 17 months. Cynthia lives in Lewes with her husband.

Judy Catterton, a retired Washington, D.C. area trial lawyer, currently teaches memoir and essay writing for the Rehoboth Beach Writers' Guild. In 2015, the Delaware Division of the Arts named her Individual Artist Fellow for non-fiction writing. Her essays have appeared in literary journals including: *Alligator/Juniper* (contest finalist); *Noise* (Grand Prize); *Chatter House Press* (third prize) and *The Ravens' Perch*. Her poems have appeared in *Beach Life Magazine, Third Wednesday* and *Rat's Ass Review*.

Terri Clifton is an enthusiastic writer of both fiction and non-fiction. Her short stories have appeared in several anthologies including the award-winning Beach Reads series, *Rehoboth Reimagined*, and *The Divine Feminine*. She is the author of *A Random Soldier*, a memoir, and was awarded the 2013 Emerging Artist Fellowship in Fiction Literature by the Delaware Division of Arts.

Ellen Collins is the author of two volumes of poetry: *The Memory Thief* and *Invitations: Poems of Yoga and Meditation*. She has published in several books and journals including *The Divine Feminine: An Anthology of Seaside Scribes, Rehoboth Reimagined*, and *The Bellevue Literary Review*. Ellen is an active member of the Rehoboth Beach Writers' Guild and divides her time between Vienna, Virginia and Bethany Beach, Delaware.

Gail Braune Comorat is a founding member of Rehoboth Beach Writers' Guild, and the author of *Phases of the Moon* (Finishing Line Press). She has twice received DDOA fellowship grants for poetry. Her work has appeared in *Gargoyle, Grist, Mudfish, Philadelphia Stories*, and *The Widows' Handbook*. She's a long-time member of several writing groups in Rehoboth Beach, Delaware.

Ginny Daly is a lifelong writer since winning a Campbell Soup writing contest at age 10. Her agency Daly Direct Marketing's clients included the Smithsonian, National Geographic, Washington Post, Time-Life-Books and others. Her book "Guestiquette" gives useful tips for house-guests and hosts. She lives in Rehoboth Beach, Delaware and Washington, D.C. with her husband, two large Labradoodles and houseguests a'plenty!

Kelsey Dugan is a growing poet, Mama of two, cyclist and 21st century hippie. Her writing journey ignited when she was connected with the Rehoboth Beach Writers' Guild in 2013. Kelsey is currently in the process of finding her place in both the literary world and motherhood.

Mimi S Dupont spent years writing reportage and features for newspapers as well as advertising copy, public relations releases, organizational documents, state and national grant proposals, a dissertation and parent notes to teachers. She now writes poetry, personal essays and other creative nonfiction pieces of her choice. She lives halfway between Dagsboro, Delaware, and the eastern edge of the continent.

Beth Ewell grew up on Long Island and moved to Lewes, Delaware, in 1975. She is a registered nurse who retired and followed her dream to write. A member of the Rehoboth Beach Writers' Guild and student in Judy Catterton's memoir class, Beth's work has appeared in *Pulse: Voices from the Heart of Medicine*.

Linda Federman began her writing journey at *TDC: The Magazine of The Discovery Channel*. While raising two sons, her path wound her through many writing and editing roles. Linda and her husband of over thirty years are transitioning to full-time life at the beach, where—with the support of wonderful women writers in Delaware—she is reviving her focus on telling her stories.

Rosa María Fernández was born in Santa Clara, Cuba and immigrated to the United States with her family in 1965. She received a Master's degree in Social Work from The University of Maryland and is a retired psychotherapist. She lives in Lewes, Delaware with her partner, Trish, three dogs and a very moody cat. She was first published in *The Divine Feminine: An Anthology of Seaside Scribes* in 2017.

Irene Fick earned first place awards from the National Federation of Press Women and Delaware Press Association for her first collection of poetry, *The Stories We Tell (*Broadkill Press). Her poetry has been published in *Gargoyle; Poet Lore; Mojave River Review; The Broadkill Review and Philadelphia Stories.* Irene's second book, *The Wild Side of the Window,* was published by Main Street Rag in 2018.

Stephanie Fowler won the 2001 Sophie Kerr Prize at Washington College in Chestertown, Maryland, for a collection of creative non-fiction short stories about Delmarva. She owns Salt Water Media, a self-publishing company where she works with other writers and authors. Stephanie lives with her wife, Patty, in southern Delaware with their definitely-not-spoiled dog. She is currently working on her second book.

Katherine Gekker has had her poems published in *Little Patuxent Review, Broadkill Review, Poetry South, Apple Valley Review,* and elsewhere. Two composers have set her poems to music: "…to Cast a Shadow Again" by Eric Ewazen, and "Chasing the Moon Down" by Carson Cooman. Gekker's poetry collection, *In Search of Warm Breathing Things,* is forthcoming in 2019 by Glass Lyre Press.

Lisa Graff has been published in *Woman's World Magazine, The Washington Post, Delaware Beach Life Magazine, The Gaithersburg Gazette,* and many other newspapers. Her column Retirement 101 has been a bi-weekly feature in the Cape Gazette since 2012. In April 2017, Lisa published her first novel, *Find Me Alone,* available at BrowseAbout books and Amazon.com.

Crystal Heidel is an award-winning mystery novelist, freelance graphic designer, and artist who divides her time between writing, reading, and traveling to all corners of the globe. She loves food and art and has a fondness for trying new things—in writing or in real life. She's a member of the Rehoboth Beach Writers' Guild.

jahill, Jane Hill, a native of New England, retired, mother of five, resides with her guide dog on Delmarva's Eastern Shore. Writing has been a life-long exercise trying to make sense of life's complexities. The author of two collections of poetry, *i wave to the moon,* 2014, and *journey to dance,* 2015, she is currently working on her third collection, and a children's book called *friend.*

Margaret Farrell Kirby is a member of the Rehoboth Beach Writers' Guild. A memoir piece and two short stories of hers have been published in *Beach Life, The Boardwalk,* and *The Beach House.* Her poetry appeared in *The Divine Feminine: An Anthology of Seaside Scribes.* She is appreciative of Kathleen Martens and Deborah Rolig for their support and empowerment of women in the arts.

Jane Klein is a new writer and member of the Rehoboth Beach Writers' Guild, currently taking the memoir class. Jane moved to Rehoboth Beach in 2006 to change careers, now owning a local shoe store. She hopes her sons and grandchildren will gain new insight into their family history from the memoir she is currently writing.

Mary Leach, a member of the Ocean City Library Writer's Group, lives in Baltimore City, Maryland and Bethany Beach, Delaware. A PhD in mathematics, prior to her retirement, she served as a faculty member and administrator at several campuses of the University System of Maryland. She and her spouse Ron enjoy travel, reading and playing with their three grandchildren.

Faith Lord, artist and writer is a member of Rehoboth Beach Writers' Guild, as well as several art leagues, including The Ocean City Center for the Arts. "I HATE RAIN," published in 2014 *Delaware Review,* is just one stitch in her blanket of life growing up as the eldest of seven siblings and was also published in *The Divine Feminine: An Anthology of Seaside Scribes.*

Kathleen L. Martens recently won second place in the 2018 Delaware Press Association Communications Contest, for editing *The Divine Feminine,* the first Seaside Scribes anthology. Her short stories also took first and third place, and appeared in *Delaware Beach Life* magazine, Rehoboth Beach Reads series by Cat and Mouse Press, and *Rehoboth Reimagined,* published by the Rehoboth Beach Writers' Guild—her source of writing inspiration and skills.

Rita B. Nelson is a retired Episcopal priest and a member of the Rehoboth Beach Writers' Guild. Her first book, a memoir, *Always Kristen,* details her journey with her transgender daughter. She devotes herself to writing her next book, a novel, and genealogy research. She lives with her husband, daughter, and Maltese dog, Loki, in Millsboro. Read her blog at www.wordsfromthecrone.com.

Annie Plowman started writing around the same time she learned how to walk. As a member of the Rehoboth Beach Writers' Guild with a double major in English and Journalism, Annie actively uses her love for language to express experiences we all have, but don't always know how to put into words.

Carole Schauer is a retired psychiatric nurse and lives in Ocean Pines, Maryland. Volunteer work, reading, writing, golfing, bowling, and traveling are among her interests. She enjoys writing essays about experiences in her life and that of family and friends. She is a member of the Ocean City Writers' Group.

Nancy Powichroski Sherman has been a teacher for over 43 years, but a writer since she was old enough to sit at her bedroom window and imagine. Her short stories have been published in *Delaware Beach Life*, *Fox Chase Review*, *Referential*, *The Beach House*, *Rehoboth Reimagined*, and last year's *The Divine Feminine* anthology, as well as her own collection of stories, *Sandy Shorts*.

Irene Emily Wanberg I am a very friendly Norwegian, Irish, 3% Jew, 35-year-old female who loves works of art, walking in the wilderness, composing poetry, and listening to indie, jazz, blues, folk and modern musical artists. I live in Princess Anne, Maryland, and will be studying at the university to earn a Masters of Education and to specialize my study in the realm of Art Therapy.

Marjorie F. Weber began her career as a journalist and later was a technical writer for 25 years. Her work has appeared in *The Divine Feminine*, *Delmarva Review*, *Delaware Beach Life*, and *Rehoboth Reimagined*. In 2013, she received a DDOA fellowship as an emerging artist in creative nonfiction. She is an active member of the Rehoboth Beach Writers' Guild.

Katherine Winfield, a part-time resident of Bethany Beach, Delaware, is the author of the Corsica Series, *Haverford House* and *Belle Grove*, acclaimed mysteries set on the Eastern Shore. Her books are available on Amazon and local bookstores. *Bending Toward the Light*, her latest novel is due out summer 2018. For more information about the author go to www.katherinewinfield.com.

Judy Wood splits her time between Washington, D.C. and Rehoboth Beach, Delaware. A retired Chinese Antique Dealer, she also spent three years living in Stockholm, Sweden as the wife of the Ambassador from the United States to Sweden. Several years ago, she joined the Rehoboth Beach Writers' Guild. When not entertaining or being entertained by one of her eight grandchildren, she is STILL writing a novel.

Sherri Wright lives in Rehoboth Beach, Delaware after a career in education at universities and the federal government. Running, practicing yoga, working out, and volunteering at a center for the homeless all figure into her writing. A member of Rehoboth Beach Writers' Guild and Key West Poetry Guild, her poems and essays have appeared in a variety of journals and anthologies.

CPSIA information can be obtained
at www.ICGtesting.com
Printed in the USA
FSHW02n2326150818
51309FS